A Widow's Might

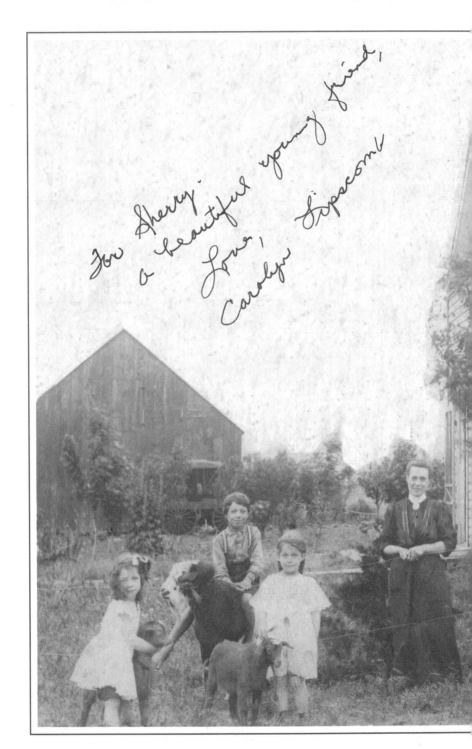

For Sherry -
a beautiful young friend,
Love,
Carolyn Lipscomb

A Widow's Might

Carolyn Ellis Lipscomb

Magnolia
Mansions
Press

Library of Congress Catalog Card Number: 99-63995
ISBN 0-9665175-3-9

Printed in the United States of America

Design and production, Bob & Faith Nance
Cover photography, Mary Wood Littleton

Jacket: The quilt pictured on the jacket was presented to Mattie Norman Ellis in 1985 by her children and grandchildren. It was her most cherished possession.

Magnolia Mansions Press
4661 Pinewood Drive
Mobile, AL 36618
Boellis25@aol.com

This true story
is lovingly dedicated to
the memory of my parents,
The Reverend Henry Marvin and Mattie Norman Ellis,
and to the generous benefactor
who changed Mama's life.
May he be remembered with respect and gratitude.

Contents

$\mathscr{P}$reface

THIS IS A TRUE STORY. WITH THE HELP OF daily journals, family letters, letters from friends, newspaper accounts, personal interviews, and court records, I have strived for accuracy in telling the story of my mother, Mattie Norman Ellis, how she dealt with widowhood and adversity, and how she was rewarded in the end. Many of the records were written by Mama. She and I (since I was the only one of her children living in Auburn at the time) were the two people most closely involved in the research and recording of events leading up to the trial.

It concerns mostly Mama's bequest from Mr. Reuben Cowart*, what led him to name her as his beneficiary, and subsequent events which were exciting and gratifying but at the same time very stressful. In an attempt to avoid embarrassment for members of some of the families involved in this account, I have changed a number of names and locales.

The title, *A Widow's Might*, suggests Mama's strengths. She was a person of might in every facet of her life—her integrity, her morals, and her determination to keep her children together in spite of overwhelming odds and her perseverance as a true southern lady. Another title I considered, *Where There's a Will*,

---

*Not his real name.

The names of many of the key characters have been changed. These will be indicated by an asterisk when first introduced.

There's a Way, had a twofold implication: Mr. Cowart's Last Will and Testament certainly is a major factor in this story, and Mama's will to keep her children together is equally important.

This is a significant part of our family history. Some years ago I brought up something about Mr. Reuben Cowart, and our son Lan said "I always thought that was a 'no-no' subject." I was dismayed that one of our children had that mistaken idea, and I assured him that it was not a taboo subject in the least, and the only reason we had not discussed it with our children earlier was because they were too young to understand. Caroline, Lan, and James were seven, five and three respectively when this occurred, and Katherine was born four years later.

I emphasized the fact that there was nothing about these events to make our family ashamed. On the contrary, it was one of the most exciting things that had ever happened to us, and the overwhelming support that Mama received from friends as well as acquaintances was richly gratifying. Certainly we learned in a very dramatic way that Mama was greatly admired and that those who knew her well would not allow her integrity or her morals to be questioned. Recalling these events made me realize more than ever what a remarkable person Mama was. It also renewed my awareness of the sad, sad life Mr. Cowart endured. I'm glad that our family apparently brought some pleasure into his life. He certainly shed happiness in ours, and I hope this story will always be a reminder to my family to think of him with affection and gratitude.

Acknowledgments

A REMARK BY MY SON LAN MOTIVATED ME TO write this story of my mother, Mattie Norman Ellis. In addition to providing the impetus I needed for this undertaking, he has spent many hours proofreading and editing, suggesting changes and improvements in word usage and correcting my somewhat outdated punctuation, but he never failed to encourage me. He deserves much of the credit for bringing my manuscript to a point where it could become a book.

As I delved into the recesses of my mind, and also into the recesses of the many boxes that Mama had stored in closets and cupboards, I discovered that remembering one event often triggered other memories. My brother Wesley has verified many of the facts and has added valuable information and memories of his own. In fact, he was directly involved in writing about events in this book of which I had little or no knowledge. There were times when our memories seemed so in tune that it was almost spooky. For example, when I called to suggest that he write about his experience as a concert organist in Costa Rica he was already in the process of writing it.

In addition to Lan and Wesley, my daughters, Caroline and Katherine, my son James, my niece Jeanne Robertson, and my friend Mabel Caley Kelley Carlton have all encouraged me to continue writing and to find a way to publish this story if possible. Jeanne, who has several books in print, has given me valuable information and advice on publishing as well as timely boosts of encouragement when I appeared to be "dragging my feet."

My friends Patsy and Bob Holman and Phyllis and Bruce Martin, all successful authors, have given me helpful advice. Phyllis suggested the name *A Widow's Might*, and my friend Jay Sanders suggested *Where There's a Will, There's a Way*, which I have used for the titles of two of the chapters.

Jack Simms, journalist and author of several books, as well as a friend of many years, has offered valuable professional advice and assistance. Mary Littleton's expertise with a camera and sophisticated equipment has resulted in enhanced vintage pictures throughout the manuscript. She has graciously shared her considerable talents in this area. Jay Lamar is another talented young friend who has contributed greatly to the final shaping of this book. She is an excellent editor as well as an encourager.

Without the help of these and many others my efforts would have flagged a long time ago. I am grateful for those who read my manuscript at different stages of its development, and most of all, for the many notes and expressions of encouragement. In each of these I discovered a depth of admiration for Mama that increased my resolve to continue writing.

Many of the people who so willingly shared their support during that stressful period preceding and during the trial are no longer alive. I will always remember them with gratitude, and I hope their descendants will take pride in their acts of kindness.

The generous benefactor who changed Mama's life and Mama, whose strength of character motivated him to bring about this change, are the central figures in the most exciting part of this story. Mama was greatly admired during her lifetime and I believe that she is still revered by those who remember her. I hope that this story will serve as a reminder to the reader that Mr. Cowart was also a person to be admired and respected, a kind and generous man who expected nothing in return.

Mattie Norman, 1919

Henry Marvin Ellis, 1932

One
A Young
Widow

Daddy, the Reverend Henry Marvin Ellis, was sick when we moved from Centreville to Eutaw, Alabama, in November 1932. He never even preached a sermon in the Eutaw Methodist Church, although we lived in the parsonage there almost two years.

At first it appeared that he had pneumonia, and then his doctor decided that it might be pleurisy, or lung cancer, or, more likely, a lung abscess. This was before the days of antibiotics, so the outcome would probably have been the same, whatever the diagnosis. He was sick for four months at Vaughn Memorial Hospital in Selma before he died on March 31, 1933. I was three years old—almost four—and I yearn for memories of my father.

The people in Eutaw, and especially the members of the Methodist Church, were caring and compassionate. The church's district presiding elder had arranged for a minister serving a nearby church to also serve Eutaw. He was already living in the parsonage of his primary church, so our family was allowed to remain in the Eutaw parsonage. I don't remember the name of the interim preacher, but we called him Brother H. and he had a wooden leg. My brothers, Howard, Norman, and Wesley, were fascinated by his leg, and especially since Brother H. demonstrated the way to take it off and then put it back on.

Mama stayed with Daddy during his illness, day and night, going briefly each day to freshen up and get some rest at the home of one of his doctors, Dr. Grayson, who lived directly across the street from the hospital. Mama wrote in her journal, "While we were at the hospital a great many people did so many thoughtful things for us. How I wish I could enumerate all of them. His doctors were attentive to Marvin's every need, and we could not have asked for better medical care.

"When I learned that Marvin was going to die, I told his doctors that I had no money, but that I would pay the bills when I collected Marvin's life insurance. None of those wonderful doctors charged for their services, and the hospital charged only the flat room fee—not a dime for X-rays, lab work, or other expenses. When I asked about my meals, I learned that the members of the Orrville Methodist Church, which Marvin had served, paid for them weekly with butter, eggs, milk, chickens, and vegetables from their gardens. [This was during the Depression when people had very little money, but nearly everyone grew their own vegetables, kept a cow to milk, and raised chickens.]

"I had a cot in Marvin's room and stayed there every night except one, when Dr. Sam Kirkpatrick sensed that I was near the breaking point so he insisted that I sleep in a nearby hospital room. I was given a sedative and I slept through the night. Dr. Kirkpatrick, an ophthalmologist, was not one of Marvin's doctors, but he dropped by almost every day for a visit. He was a saintly man—a staunch Methodist—and he was a source of strength for both Marvin and me."

Daddy and Mama came home briefly for Christmas of 1932 and then returned to Selma. Many years later Mama wrote, "We left very early in the morning to go back to the hospital, and I had told the children the night before that we would not awaken them. However, the three older ones, Gay, Howard, and Norman, insisted that they wanted to get up to see us off. As we drove away, Gay and Norman were on the front steps waving and calling out 'have a good trip,' but Howard was walking around the side of the house with his arm across his eyes—the most dejected little boy one could imagine. That sight has stayed in my mind all these years, and I have thought of it many times since Howard's untimely death in 1979."

Our grandmother and Mama's younger sister, Aunt Alma, stayed with us part of the time, and Daddy's sister, Aunt Lena, took a turn too. After Christmas some wonderful families from the churches Daddy had served took over the care of all of us children. At first all six of us stayed with the A. F. Caleys in Marion Junction. I don't remember that visit, but I went back to visit the Caleys many times after that. They were a dear couple, and they made us feel welcome and loved in their beautiful two-story farm house with lots of room to play, horses to ride, and abundant, delicious food to eat.

Their daughter, Mabel, was sixteen years old, and my five-year-old brother Wesley thought she was beautiful. He confessed many years later that when Mabel left with a group of teenage friends one night, he hid behind a forsythia bush and wept bitter tears of jealousy.

After a few weeks with the Caleys, Mama's three girls, Gay, Lamar, and I, stayed with Mr. and Mrs. Floyd Farish in Orrville. Mrs. Farish's mother lived with them and she was a loving surrogate grandmother for us. Her name was Mrs. I. D. Wilson but we called her "Idee" and we adored her. She usually wore an apron and sometimes she would hide surprises for us in her apron pockets. She hummed softly as she rocked, first Lamar and then me in her big wicker rocking chair. All of these generous people who cared for us remained close friends through the years, and even now the second and third generations of the Caley family have remained close.

Several years ago I learned that Mrs. Farish was in a nursing home in Selma, and I went by to see her, never dreaming that she would know who I was. She was sitting quietly in her wheelchair, and when I leaned over and said, "Mrs. Farish, I'm Carolyn Ellis Lipscomb," she immediately reached up to hug me with tears in her eyes. I thanked her for taking care of me when I was a small child, and we sat quietly holding hands, both of us crying and remembering more than sixty years ago. There was little conversation, but it was a time of gentle communication for her and me, and I will never forget it.

During Daddy's illness, Mama and Mrs. T. J. Jackson became very close and lifelong friends. It would have been customary in those days for them to address each other as "Mrs. Ellis" and "Mrs. Jackson," but that was not the case with Mama and Mrs. Jackson. Her name was Cola Barr and that is what she wanted to be called, and she always addressed Mama as Mattie.

The Jacksons were Presbyterians, but as soon as Cola Barr heard about the Methodist preacher who was desperately sick and his young wife who was staying with him, she came to the hospital to help. They lived near the hospital and Mrs. Jackson came to see Mama nearly every day, sometimes several times a day. She was a happy-natured person and her positive attitude helped keep Mama's spirits up. There were seven children in the Jackson family and sometimes Mrs. Jackson would invite the "three little ones"—Wesley, Lamar, and me—to spend the day with her three youngest children, John Munford, Jo, and Sally. These visits would give Mama an opportunity to spend a little time with her children without being away from the hospital too long. The Jacksons had a huge white three-story house with a cupola on top. We loved to climb all those flights of steps to the very top where we could walk around in the cupola, and I thought we could see the whole wide world from up there. Many years later I learned with disappointment that that beautiful old home had been demolished and replaced by an apartment building.

Mama kept a little notebook by Daddy's hospital bed in which she recorded names of visitors and those who sent flowers. There were over thirty Methodist ministers listed, in addition to numerous other friends. On February 19, 1933, she wrote, "Today is my thirty-third birthday and our thirteenth anniversary. Lena [one of Daddy's sisters] and the children came to see us and brought gifts. Mama [our grandmother] sent a pair of silk hose, Gay brought a little wire basket, Mrs. Wilson sent a box of food, and Mrs. Farish two linen handkerchiefs for an anniversary gift for Marvin and me." The next entry, other than lists of names, was dated March 2, 1933: "Marvin has just finished praying the most beautiful prayer. He was irrational at the time and was suffering but made no reference whatever to pain or suffering. Among other things he thanked God for his faithful wife and precious children, for a Christian home and that he had been called into His service, also for a place in His kingdom to work. He prayed for a supply of grace sufficient for each day's need and then finished by saying, 'And then when we have come to the end of the way, may we, on angel's wings, be wafted to that Bright City whose builder and maker is God. Amen.'"

Then Mama quoted the following poem:

Not until each loom is silent
And the shuttles cease to fly,
Will God unroll the pattern
And explain the reason why.
The dark threads are as needful
In the Weaver's skillful hand

5

As the threads of gold and silver
For the pattern which he planned.
                              (Author unknown)

She ended her entry by quoting from Norman B. Harrison's
His Peace, the Way of Living Without Worrying:

> Our life is like the dial of a clock. The hands are God's
> hands passing over and over again. The short hand, the Hand
> of Discipline; the long hand, the Hand of Mercy. Slowly and
> surely the Hand of Discipline must pass and God speaks at
> each stroke, but over and over passes the Hand of Mercy
> showering down sixtyfold of blessings for each stroke of Dis-
> cipline. Both hands are fastened to one secure pivot, the
> Great, Unchanging Heart of a God of Love.

DADDY DIED MARCH 31, 1933, AFTER STRUGGLING with his
illness for four long months. Wesley remembers Mrs. Caley
gently breaking the news to him, and then holding him close
as he grieved over a loss that he was too young to understand.
Lamar and I were not quite two and four and don't remember
any of the circumstances, but I'm sure the two oldest children,
Gay and Howard, never forgot that sad time, and Norman still
remembers it vividly.

Miss Ruth Davis, the head nurse at the hospital, was a great
source of gentle comfort and attention to Mama and Daddy.
After Daddy's death she told Mama, "Brother Ellis did more good
on his death bed than any preacher I have ever known by his
uncomplaining acceptance of pain, and his appreciation for everything that was done for him."

Our family gathered at the Jackson home before Daddy's funeral. The service was at Church Street Methodist Church and
burial was in the Jacksons' lot at New Live Oak Cemetery. They

Mama and Norman, Wesley, Gay, Howard, Lamar, and Carolyn at Daddy's grave, April 4, 1933

had a large lot, and Mrs. Jackson knew that Mama had no money to buy one, so they very generously gave her space for Daddy's grave and reserved the space next to him for Mama's burial place. Uncle Frank Ellis and his daughter, Katherine, were among the relatives who came to the funeral. Katherine was seventeen at the time, and she told me that more than sixty years later she still has a vivid memory of Wesley, Lamar, and me sitting on the stairway at the Jackson home as they were saying their goodbyes. Katherine had forgotten her coat, and when she ran back in the house to get it she looked up at us, sitting with our elbows on our knees and holding our heads with looks of sadness and bewilderment. The three of us did not go to the funeral because we were too young, but I know we went to the cemetery later that day because we have a picture of Mama with all six of us children standing there looking down at the flowers covering Daddy's grave.

MAMA WAS BORN FEBRUARY 19, 1900, SO IT WAS EASY to remember her age. Whatever the year, that's how old she was, and

7

Howard, Gay, and Norman, August 1926

Daddy with Carolyn in front of the Pine Apple parsonage, 1930

Mama, Gay, Norman, and Howard, August 1926

Daddy and Gay with the Centreville parsonage in the background, 1932

Norman, Howard, and Wesley with their little dog, Mitzi, in Centreville, 1932

she was only 33 years old with six young children when Daddy died. Gay was twelve, the three boys came next—Howard, Norman, and Wesley—I was next to the youngest at almost four, and finally Lamar, who was almost two. This was during the Depression and Mama had little money and almost no furniture because we had lived in parsonages. But she did have abundant determination and intelligence.

She had completed a business course when she was eighteen years old, two years before she and Daddy married. Her brother, Howard, was dismayed when he learned that their mother had made Mama quit high school shortly before she was to graduate, and Grandma insisted that Mama take a job in a dry goods store in their hometown, State Line, Mississippi, in order to help with their family expenses. Mama pleaded with her to let her work in the afternoons after school until she could finish school. Grandma was adamant, and Mama wrote Uncle Howard about her frustrations and disappointment. Uncle Howard recognized her capabilities and her determination to make something better of her life. Grandma did not give in on many things, but Uncle Howard convinced her that she must relent and let Mattie prepare herself for something more in line with her abilities. He arranged for her to take a business course, and he paid all of her expenses, an arrangement which made it easier for Grandma to accept.

Mama and three other young ladies roomed and boarded at the home of their teacher, Miss Allie Kate Suttle, in Meridian, Mississippi. By studying sixteen to eighteen hours a day, Mama completed the course in typing and shorthand in two months. She was a whiz as a secretary. Her little hands flew over the keyboard of her Underwood manual typewriter, typing 120 words a minute, and she took dictation at an incredible speed. Mama always apologized for her handwriting, which was legible but not pretty. She said that learning shorthand had ruined her longhand, but she was comparing it to Daddy's, which was beautiful Spencerian script.

Miss Suttle placed her students in the best jobs she could find for them. Mama went to work as secretary to the president of the bank in Chatom, Alabama, where she also filled in as a teller from time to time. Daddy was not yet a preacher then but was a bookkeeper for the E.E. Jackson Lumber Company nearby, and he came to the bank nearly every day to take care of the lumber company's business. He came even more frequently after he met Mattie Norman, a pretty little brunette who refused to go out with him at first because she thought he was much too old for her. He was a bachelor, almost sixteen years older than she, but he finally won her over, and they were married on her twentieth birthday, February 19, 1920.

Daddy made the decision to go into the Methodist ministry, following in the footsteps of his father and grandfather, soon after he and Mama married.

THOUGH ONLY FIVE FEET TALL AND WEIGHING 100 pounds when she married, Mama had boundless energy and fierce determination to make up for her small size. She weighed 106 pounds after Lamar was born, saying that she gained one pound for each of her six children. She later gained enough weight that she would be described as plump. Her dark brown hair was usually pulled back from her face, calling attention to her piercing blue eyes. Those eyes never seemed to waver, always looking intently at whomever she might be in conversation with. If any of her children misbehaved or failed to carry out an assignment, her eyes conveyed her disapproval. At the same time she could just as readily convey affection and pride if we did something that pleased her.

Mama did not write in her journal every day, although she tried to record enough to help her remember important events

*Mama with Carolyn, Norman,
and Wesley, December 1929*

and turning points. After she was told that Daddy would not
recover from his illness she wrote, "I spent many hours agoniz-
ing about the future and how I would manage to keep my children together. It never one time occurred to me that they would
be separated—the question was simply, 'How would I manage?'
Suddenly, one day, a strange sensation came over me—a feeling
of calmness and assurance. I felt as if someone was saying, 'There
will be a way.' From that time on, I had no doubt."

She was determined to keep us all together, though several
people approached her with other options. Even before Daddy
was buried, Aunt Alma and Uncle Emory offered to take "either
Norman or the two little girls" (Lamar and me), and when Mama
told them that she intended to keep us all together, Aunt Alma
called her a "damn fool."

Dr. Monroe Maas, one of the doctors who had been so wonderful to Mama and Daddy throughout their long stay in Selma, told Mama that he and his wife wanted very much to adopt Lamar and me and that they would love us and give us every opportunity possible. He was Jewish and his wife Methodist, and he said that they would raise us as Methodists. One of the nurses, Miss Ruth Davis, told Mama that Dr. Maas was one of the most generous contributors to the Church Street Methodist Church, which his wife and daughter attended, but he remained loyal to the Jewish faith. He was quoted as saying that he would not hurt his mother by leaving the Jewish faith as long as she lived. Dr. and Mrs. Maas had one child, a daughter, Jean, who was about twelve or thirteen years old. Mama wrote, "I never met his daughter, but if she is as gentle and kind as her father, she should have a host of friends for he was wonderful."

In her journal Mama wrote, "Since it was during the Great Depression of the 1930s, Dr. Maas, as most people, assumed that it would be impossible for me to keep my children together—apparently few people knew that I had had good secretarial training and experience and that I was determined not to separate the children. A prominent businessman from Gastonburg told Miss Davis the same thing—he and his wife wanted the two little girls, or if not, any two of the other children."

Since I have been an adult, I have realized that Lamar and I were the first choices for would-be adoptive parents because we were the youngest, not because we were prettier or sweeter or smarter than our older siblings. If any of these people could have predicted the future, I believe that Wesley would have been their first choice because he is not only intelligent but tremendously talented as well. During the years when Mama struggled so, I wonder if she regretted her decision not to accept the generous offers of those two couples.

MANY YEARS LATER WESLEY AND I, along with my daughter
Caroline and her infant daughter, Katherine, met Jean Maas
Johnson, a beautiful, lovely lady who still lives in Selma. She
generously shared memories of her parents and of others whom
Mama had referred to in her journal. She had not known of her
father's offer to adopt us, but she did not seem surprised. She
told us that he died when she was only sixteen, just three years
after my father's death.

WHEN WE RETURNED TO EUTAW AFTER THE FUNERAL we were
surrounded by relatives and friends, all well-meaning and helpful, but Mama was so exhausted and so relieved to be with her
children once again after being away from us for months that
she wanted only a much-needed rest and some time with us.

Easter was less than two weeks away, and preparations were
underway for the church's Easter program. The chairman of the
program committee asked Mama if I could recite a little poem,
so of course Mama agreed and made sure that I learned it:

> *A Little Lily*
>
> *I'm but a little lily,*
> *Like this that I hold forth,*
> *But Mama says I'm sweeter*
> *Than any flower on earth.*
>
> *She says, if I am always*
> *As sweet as I am now, that I*
> *Shall meet the risen Savior*
> *In Heaven by and by.*

Mama wrote, "Carolyn recited this poem in the Easter program at the Eutaw Methodist Church on April 16, 1933, just 16
days after her daddy's death and nine days before her fourth

Carolyn, Lamar, and Wesley on the steps of the Eutaw Methodist Church, August 1933

birthday. She wore the little green silk dress that I made for the picture of her and Lamar which was taken shortly before Marvin's death. She held an Easter lily and recited every word of the poem. There were few dry eyes as the congregation was aware of the sadness in our family."

I cannot speak for Mama or her older children, but for me life turned quickly again to that mix of play, wonder, and contentment which forms my earliest recollections.

In a house nearby lived an older couple and their adult daughter. We wouldn't have even been interested in knowing more about them, but Gay, my oldest sister, heard that the husband and his wife had not spoken to each other in at least fifteen years. Of course Gay wanted to know more about that. The parents and their daughter, Virginia, would sit at the dinner table and Mr. H. would say, "Virginia, tell your mother to pass the salt and pepper." Or Mrs. H. would say, "Virginia, ask your father what he did with the newspaper." Poor Virginia would pass messages back and forth when her parents were sitting right there at the table, and they already knew what had been said. We tried every way we could think of to peep in that house and observe these strange happenings. Howard even lifted me up on his shoulders, hoping that I could make a firsthand report, but if I saw or heard anything I think my ability to report it would have been unreliable. I don't even remember all this, but I heard about it from Gay and Howard.

We had a lot of playmates in the neighborhood near the parsonage, and the churchyard was a wonderful place to play. Once there was a fair or carnival near the parsonage. It had a huge ferris wheel, or at least it seemed huge to me. One of my few vivid memories of Eutaw involved that ferris wheel, and it contributed to my lifelong fear of all carnival rides, with the exception of merry-go-rounds. As each car of the ferris wheel was loaded, it was sent upward until a vacant car appeared on the loading platform. A large black woman panicked when she was seated in a swinging car that was stopped at the very top. She apparently was rocking back and forth in her hysteria, and that caused the car to swing violently. She let out a piercing scream, released the safety bar, and jumped to the ground! I have never forgotten that scream or the resounding thud when she hit the ground. The adults were frantically trying to get all the children away from there, but we saw the woman as she was loaded on a stretcher and carried away. Later I asked Mama what had happened to her, and she assured me that she had nothing worse than a broken leg. Mama wouldn't have lied to me, but she probably would have spared me from knowing if anything more serious had occurred.

Another deep-seated fear that I have never been able to overcome is a fear of snakes. Just writing that word, s-n-a-k-e, makes me shudder with horror even now, more than six decades after my brother Howard caused me to have this phobia. He loved to tease me, knowing that I was gullible and naive, and I was the victim of many of his practical jokes. One day he told me that he had a surprise for me and to close my eyes and hold out my hands. Like a fool, I did just what he told me to do, and he dropped a little green snake, cold and wriggly, in my hands. I screamed hysterically and spent the rest of the day endlessly washing my hands and sobbing uncontrollably. I would not eat anything because I didn't want to touch food or anything else with my contaminated hands. I watched for Mama to come home from work that afternoon and as soon as I saw her, I rushed into her arms and told her about Howard's dastardly deed. I'm sure she gave Howard a tongue-lashing, and he probably appeared somewhat contrite, but I don't think he really was. I'm not even sure that Mama thought it was such a terrible prank because she wasn't afraid of snakes and other slimy critters, but she probably was upset that he had caused me to be so frightened. Howard continued to find ways to tease me, even after we were adults, but that was the thing that had the most lasting effect on me.

This picture of Lamar and Carolyn was taken in March 1933, shortly before Daddy died. He kept it by his bedside. (A gift from Mr. and Mrs. Floyd Farish.)

Mama, Lamar, and Carolyn in Centreville, 1932

Two
Rest and Renewal

G[AY, H]OWARD, AND N[ORMAN WERE ALL IN SCHOOL] until the end of May. Mr. and Mrs. Murphy McMillan (Cap'n Murph and Miss Lillie) who lived in Stockton, Alabama, invited us to come for a visit as soon as the school term ended.

Mama was devoted to the McMillan family, and through the years she often spoke of their love and support during Daddy's ministry in Stockton. Mrs. McMillan's gentle and generous spirit is evident in the following letter which she sent to Mama and which Mama saved as a treasured remembrance:

April 9, 1933
My Dear Mrs. Ellis,

Certainly the passing of Mr. Ellis in the prime of his beautiful, useful life, which seemed to us so necessary—not only to his family but to the advancement of the cause of Christ— is one of the profound mysteries which only Heaven can explain. But we do know that our Father is a God of love and wisdom and that He cannot make a mistake....

I know that Heaven seems so near to you as you realize

19

that the faithful companion who has shared the joys and sorrows of this life, is now basking in the sunlight of God's presence and looking forward to the coming of his wife and children.

Can't you and the children come and spend a while with us? We have plenty of room for every one of you, shall be glad to have you; and feel that you owe it to yourself and children to have a complete rest before taking up the broken threads of life.

I am sure that God will provide a way whereby you and your children will be cared for without being separated....Please write me at once when you and the children can come.

With love and deepest sympathy for you and the children.

Sincerely, your friend,
Lillie McMillan

Mama wrote of that visit, "They lived in a big rambling house. There were several Negro families living on the place—their cook had a house in the backyard—and there was an abundance of garden vegetables, chickens, eggs, and home-cured meat. Cap'n Murph and Miss Lillie insisted that we were not a burden as I had feared we might be. It was a wonderfully relaxing experience for me, and the children were happy to be on a farm with so many things to enjoy. There were young black children who loved playing with the smaller ones so I had little to do but rest, read, or visit with the many friends who came to visit us—friends and neighbors from our stay in Stockton."

The McMillans had beautiful, fine horses, but the only one I remember was Daisy, who was very old and blind as well. Ephraim, a kind and exceedingly patient black man, would put Lamar and me on poor old Daisy's back and then lead us round and round the pasture. Lamar and I thought it was exciting but it must have been extremely boring for Ephraim.

Cap'n Murph had a houseboat, and we took a cruise on the nearby Tensaw River one evening, enjoying supper on the boat and the haunting songs of the blacks singing onboard the boat as we rolled slowly along the waterway. That is my earliest memory of moonlight on the water, and I'm sure it was a beautiful, clear starlit night because it made a lasting impression on me. Even when I think of it now, I have a pleasant sensation of tranquility and beauty.

After we left the McMillans, with many happy memories to treasure, we went to State Line, Mississippi, for a few days with Grandma and with Aunt Alma and Uncle Emory, who lived nearby. We must have worn them out when they stayed with us during the early stages of Daddy's illness because I don't think we stayed there very long. I remember Uncle Emory was driving his car with all of us, including Grandma and Aunt Alma, in it. At a long, steep hill everyone except Uncle Emory had to get out and walk while he turned the car around and backed up the hill because of the slippery red clay. That always puzzled me and I wondered if I had dreamed it, but Howard explained that it made sense because reverse is the most powerful gear and back then cars had rear-wheel drive. Grandma was only four feet, ten inches tall, and I remember her as a determined, no-nonsense person. I have a vivid memory of her trudging up that long hill, her face dripping with perspiration, with her head covered with a large white handkerchief, each of the four corners tied in a knot.

Grandma was our only living grandparent, and we saw little of her during the years. She had no car and neither did Mama, but I do remember one visit to her house in State Line. She had beautiful flowers that grew in profusion all over her somewhat cluttered yard. People used to say that Clementine Norman had a green thumb and that she could root a broomstick. I kept looking at her hands hoping to see her green thumbs, but they always looked just like everyone else's. She had a large vegetable garden in the back corner of her yard. One afternoon a neighbor's cow got through the fence, evidently a not uncommon occurrence, and she was trampling row after row of the vegetables that were just about ready to pick. Grandma grabbed her shotgun and ran out yelling at the cow while spraying her with bird shot. With a look of satisfaction she said, "That'll teach that heifer to stay out of my garden." It must have worked because I don't believe she did come back, at least not as long as we were there.

The first afternoon we were at Grandma's house, she came out on the porch where we were playing and announced that supper was ready. We were startled at that because it was about four o'clock in the afternoon, but we knew better than to question anything she said. Finally, Mama asked her why we were eating so early, and Grandma said, "because we have to go to bed by dark." That puzzled us too, but at last the explanation came out. Grandma had been seriously ill earlier that year, and she spent about two months with Aunt Alma and Uncle Emory. When she got her light bill, which was the minimum amount (probably no more than one dollar), she refused to pay it because she had not even turned on a light for two months or more. She steadfastly stuck to her resolution that she would not pay for something she did not use, so the Mississippi Power Company had no choice but to turn off her electricity. She lived the rest of her life in that little house without electricity, but she always felt that she had proved her point and had taught the power company a lesson.

We went by train from State Line to Meridian where our cousin, Ellis Williamson, met us and drove us to his home nearby. His mother, Aunt Lola, was Daddy's youngest sister, and her husband, Uncle Walter, had been supportive and helpful in many ways during Daddy's illness. In addition to Ellis, they had two daughters, Edith and Neegie, who were about the ages of Gay and Howard. Mama wrote of that visit, "They were all so warm and cordial that I never felt that we were an imposition, so it is no wonder that I love each of them with a special feeling. I'll never forget Walter's kindness to me in taking care of a life insurance premium that came due during the 'Bank Holiday' and his calling me at the hospital to let me know that it had been paid on time.

"They had a nice garden, and Lola and I spent many pleasant hours sitting on the back porch shelling peas and snapping beans. Our children played well together, and the older ones gave me blessed relief by looking after my younger children. Lola always said that Marvin was her favorite brother, and she was grieving over his death just as I was."

Our last visit that summer was with Uncle Wesley and Aunt Carrie Hall in Shelby, Mississippi. Uncle Wesley, a family physician, had rheumatoid arthritis, and although he spent much of his time in a wheelchair, he still took care of his many patients. Mama wrote the following about our visit: "Our welcome to the Hall home was no less cordial than the Williamsons'. Carrie had written to me to extend an invitation to visit them, saying, 'You will not be a financial burden because we have everything except money. Just about everyone in Shelby and the surrounding area owes Dr. Hall for services, and we can have everything from dry cleaning to barber shop services. His rural patients bring us all sorts of produce, as well as chickens and eggs to apply to their bills.'"

Aunt Carrie and Uncle Wesley's two sons were also doctors: Wesley, Jr., who was elected president of the American Medical Association in 1970, and Toxey, who was an intern at Hillman Hospital in Birmingham at the time of our visit in the summer of 1933. Their sister, Elizabeth, was a teenager and she spent a lot of time with us, playing games, having tea parties, and giving

Mama an opportunity to rest and visit with Aunt Carrie and Uncle Wesley. When our visit was over, Toxey, who was returning to Birmingham, drove us all back to Eutaw. I think the car was a big black touring model. It must have been huge to accommodate our family. Toxey was a loving, happy-natured person, and with great gusto he sang funny songs as we rolled along dusty, two-lane roads—making our trip an exciting experience rather than boring or tiring. Toxey had a wonderful ability to find pleasure in everyday things, and to make us happy and cheerful.

Toxey's patients during the many years he practiced in Belzoni, Mississippi, loved him. They showed their devotion when they contributed to his "friendship wall." For the construction of his beautiful home, he had purchased old brick but it ran out before the exterior wall surrounding the house was completed. Toxey mentioned it to several of his patients, and soon people were bringing a brick or two—sometimes several—to add to his wall. He started calling it his friendship wall as a reminder of all his friends who contributed to its completion. The house began as a much smaller structure, but additions were made upstairs, in the back and on one side. It is a wonderful, unique house and it created quite a lot of interest as it took shape. One lady who was noted for her curiosity finally asked, "Dr. Hall, how many bathrooms do you plan to have?" and Toxey very smoothly replied, "We can seat six."

BACK IN EUTAW, MAMA SOON GOT A TEMPORARY job working for the Greene County Relief Office. One day Mr. Appleton, the County Agent, came by the office just before leaving for a meeting in Auburn when he said in passing, "Mrs. Ellis, is there anything I can do for you in Auburn?" and she answered, "No, thank you. I don't think so." Her office was on the second floor and as Mr. Appleton went down the steps she thought again about a realization that she had had earlier, that if she wanted

Carolyn sitting on the edge of a fishpond at the T.J. Jackson home in Selma, 1933. Lamar, Sally Jackson (in cap), and Dot Moncrief in the background.

her children to get a college education then she would need to move to a college town. On an impulse, she leaned out of the window and called out to him to see if he could find her a job in Auburn. She always said that spur-of-the-moment request was providential, and I agree.

When Mr. Appleton returned, he said, "Mrs. Ellis, I have found you a temporary job working for the Triple A [Agricultural Adjustment Administration]. I can't guarantee you anything, but I know that once they see what kind of work you do, they will not let you go." So Mama left us with a Mrs. D. while she went to Auburn for six weeks. While in Auburn Mama stayed at the home of Professor and Mrs. Walter Burkhardt, a beautiful house on the corner of Payne Street and Pinedale. Their three children, Ellwood, Beverley Ann, and Carlyle, always had a special place in Mama's heart. The Burkhardts were wonderful to her, but Mama had been away from her children during Daddy's illness and was sorry that once again it was necessary for her to leave us with others.

Mrs. Burkhardt was a quiet, gentle, and perceptive person. She sensed how much Mama longed to see her children, and she shared this feeling with her neighbors, Mrs. Alvord and Mrs.

Schrader. These three dear friends decided that one way for Mama to deal with her yearning for her children was to spend her free time in the evenings sewing for them. Mrs. Burkhardt provided space for a sewing machine which Mrs. Alvord lent her, and Mrs. Schrader contributed stacks of remnants. All three of these ladies had patterns for little girl dresses which they shared. From that time until she came back to Eutaw to move us, Mama sewed happily every evening, making clothes for her children. Many years later she related this to me, ending by saying that her friends found a way for her to cope with her homesickness, and they also provided a way for her to clothe her children and at no cost to her. The hours she spent planning, cutting, and sewing and the resulting dresses for her daughters and shirts for her sons gave Mama a sense of satisfaction in providing for her children while filling in her lonely hours.

Mrs. Schrader taught Clothing and Design in the School of Home Economics at A.P. I. (Alabama Polytechnic Institute, later named Auburn University.) She could not resist buying fabric, especially if it was on sale. Consequently she had huge stacks of remnants and dress lengths. From time to time she would be overwhelmed by her store of fabrics and decide it was time to give some of it away. She knew Mama would put it to good use, and it gave her satisfaction to donate it to a worthy cause. We later lived next door to the Schraders, and when I was in high school and then college, Mrs. Schrader was still contributing from her vast stores to Mama, many times allowing us to choose the fabrics we liked best. I can remember outfits I wore in college which were made from Mrs. Schrader's remnants.

Dr. Schrader was Professor of Chemistry at A.P. I. and he would, many years later, play an important role in one of the most exciting and traumatic events in Mama's life.

Three

The Move to Auburn

AT LAST MAMA'S SIX-WEEK TEMPORARY JOB ENDED, and she was offered a permanent position with the Agricultural Engineering Department at Alabama Polytechnic Institute. With a lot of courage and determination, she returned by train to Eutaw to get her children and her few belongings. With mounting excitement and anticipation, she walked the few blocks from the train station to the parsonage. I don't know where my older siblings were as she came in sight, but I know that Lamar and I were playing in the churchyard and we did not recognize our mother at first. She was crushed and when she related this to me many years later, I could tell that recalling her disappointment still brought tears to her eyes. I would never knowingly do anything to hurt my mother, and I'm sure she knew that a two-year-old and a four-year-old cannot be expected to react as she had hoped. How I wish that we had recognized her and that we had rushed to her embrace with outstretched arms. But sadly we didn't, and I hope we made it up to her later.

So our family of seven moved to Auburn in the fall of 1934. Mr. Nelson Grubbs, a prominent businessman in Eutaw, offered to move us since he had to go to Montevallo anyway. Mama had never had a car and had no idea where Montevallo was, but she realized later that he had gone a long way out of his way to move us. I think Mama, Gay, Wesley, Lamar, and I rode with Mr. Grubbs, and Howard and Norman rode in the truck with one of the black men from Mr. Grubbs's hardware store. I'm sure our few belongings were on that truck.

I've thought many times about Mr. Appleton and Mr. Grubbs and wish that I could remember them. Their roles in finding the job for Mama and then helping us move created a big turning point in our lives, and I'm so glad that we moved to Auburn. It is a wonderful place to live and to raise a family. All of us children attended Alabama Polytechnic Institute. My sisters and I married Auburn natives, and all of us consider "The Loveliest Village of the Plains" our home.

We knew when we were growing up that we were poor, but we never felt deprived, and Mama saw to it that we had an abundance of important dimensions in our lives that money could not buy—faith in God and commitment to our church, love of family, determination to strive to reach our limits, and a zest for life that included finding humor in everyday occurrences. She was convinced that an education was just as important for her daughters as it was for her sons.

After Mama had been a secretary in the Ag Engineering Department for a few years, the Dean of Agriculture, Marion J. Funchess, "drafted" her to be his secretary, which was a promotion for her but not much more money. Dean Funchess had a loud, booming voice, and many of the faculty and staff were intimidated by him—but not Mama. She admired him greatly and especially his ability to come right to the point, make a decision, and carry it out. She always said that he could express more thoughts in three sentences than some people could in three pages. He died in 1953 at the age of 69. The Funchesses endured two tragedies that Mama suffered over almost as if they were family members. Their grandson drowned in the goldfish pond in their backyard. It was very shallow, but I guess it doesn't take much depth for a two-year-old to drown. Their daughter, Helen, was visiting with her family, and there were several adults present—each one thinking that someone else was watching the child. Dean Funchess had the pool filled with concrete immediately after the accident. The Funchess home was on South College Street, directly across from the present site of Funchess Hall, the main building of the School of Agriculture. They had an outstanding collection of prize camellia bushes in their yard, and sometimes Mrs. Funchess would share those beautiful blooms with us. I never visited their home without looking at the filled-in pool and thinking of the precious little boy who lost his life there. The other tragedy occurred during the early 1950s when their only son, Kenneth, was lost in a plane crash in Panama. His body was never found. For years he was listed as missing in action and later officially declared killed in action.

Dr. E. V. Smith was Dean Funchess's successor and Mama continued as secretary in the Dean's office until she retired in 1964, always referring to the students in Agriculture as her boys. Many of them continued to keep in touch with her through the years and several told her that they might not have finished college if she had not encouraged them during critical times in their lives. She kept up a steady correspondence with a number of them during World War II and continued to keep in touch with them during her retirement years.

In addition to working five full days and a half day on Saturdays in the Dean's office each week, she worked many long hours typing theses and dissertations to supplement her income. She was allowed to use her typewriter at the office, staying late at night and many times going back on weekends. She always preferred an Underwood manual typewriter, and it took a while for her to adjust to the first electric one that was issued to her. There were very strict guidelines for dissertations and theses regarding margins and footnotes, and there could be no erasures or white-outs. If she made a mistake, it meant re-typing that page. There was at least one dissertation that she typed without having to re-type a single page. I've wondered many times how she would have adjusted to a word processor. When I consider how many times I have to back up and make corrections and insertions, I feel sometimes that she may be peering over my shoulder and shaking her head in disbelief: disbelief that I could make so many mistakes, but also that they could be corrected so easily on this marvelous machine.

THE FIRST HOUSE WE LIVED IN WAS AT 342 South Gay Street, and the rent was $35 a month. Mama had used some of Daddy's insurance money to buy furniture—all second-hand except the stove, mattresses, and springs—and she arranged for it to be delivered on the day we were to arrive. She wrote the following account of our arrival at the house which was to be our home: "Imagine my surprise when we drove up to the house and found all the furniture in place, shades at the windows, an icebox with ice in it, as well as milk, butter, bacon, and several other items. The kitchen table was covered with groceries. All of this was the brainchild of Lottie Grimes, the next-door neighbor, who said that she thought it would remind me of a 'Methodist pounding' which was a way of welcoming a new preacher and his family, a custom dating back for many generations. The icebox was one the Burkhardts contributed, and Professor Burkhardt had hung the window shades and curtains. Mrs. Grimes met us in the yard, picked up Lamar and took Carolyn by the hand, taking them to her house to have lunch and to play with her girls while the rest of us were unpacking and trying to get settled. I'll never forget that day or the feeling of warmth and gratitude that overcame

Mama with Gay (standing) and Carolyn and Lamar in front of their South Gay Street home in Auburn, 1937

me when we were greeted by neighbors who would become my dearest friends."

The Grimes had two little girls who were our best friends then and have remained so more than sixty years later. Mary Frances is a year younger than I, and Betty is the same age as Norman. Mary Frances, Wesley, Lamar, and I were inseparable playmates. Once when Mama offered her a piece of chocolate pie, Mary Frances answered, "No thanks, I don't eat vegetables." Chocolate pie was the most wonderful treat imaginable, and I suppose I remember that incident because I couldn't believe that anyone would turn it down.

Mama and all six of us children slept upstairs where there were two bedrooms and a small alcove. Downstairs there were two bedrooms that Mama rented to four college boys: French Sconyers, Jack Kinzer, Douglas McVay, and Oscar Bottoms. They each paid $5 a month. All of our family plus the roomers—eleven

31

people in all—shared the bathroom, which was at the end of the back porch.

Other neighbors and close friends were Shay Tidmore and her little brother Wallace, Mary Scarseth and her little brother Dwight, and also the Lowery children, John, Paul, and Mary Glenn, whom everyone called Sister. The Lowerys had a grapevine arbor in their backyard, and this provided welcome shade in the summer for our playground. Sometimes we would have Tom Thumb weddings, with Wesley usually playing the role of the preacher because he was the tallest. John Lowery was nearly always the groom because he was next-to-the tallest, and he was very handsome. Shay, Mary, and I would take turns being the bride, and Lamar was the flower girl. As soon as Sister Lowery started walking, Lamar relinquished her role as flower girl to her, and then Lamar insisted on being the bride. That pretty much put an end to the wedding season, and we started looking around for other diversions like hopscotch, Mother may I, red rover, and hide-and-go-seek.

A favorite excursion was a visit to Mrs. Alpha Cullars, Sr. who lived on the corner of Samford Avenue and South College Street. I remember her as a plump little lady with softly curling white hair, and her house always smelled deliciously like cookies baking. She greeted us with a warm smile, holding out the cookie jar for us to help ourselves. None of us were bashful, and anyway we didn't want to hurt her feelings so we probably took all our little hands would hold. We loved Mrs. Cullars, her cookies, and her pretty house. Happily that house has been spared the demolition crews that have caused many of Auburn's pretty old structures to disappear, and its appearance has changed very little since the Cullars family lived in it many years ago.

If anyone's pet died, or if we found the body of a stray animal, we made preparations to bury it with dignity and loving hands. Wesley officiated at the funerals as well as the weddings, and we all joined in the singing and praying. The little grave would be decorated with whatever flowers we could find in the neighborhood, and we searched for just the right rock to place lovingly at the head of the grave. Once, as we were digging a new grave, we inadvertently dug up the corpse of a cat that we had buried a few months earlier. It was a hideous sight, and that experience cooled our fervor for pet funerals.

We had an icebox and so did most of our neighbors. Ice was delivered by a black man called Gabe, who drove a wagon from Auburn Ice and Coal Company. The bed of the wagon was covered with sawdust and a tarpaulin shaded the large blocks of ice that were arranged on it. Gabe had huge tongs to pick up the ice, and he would carry the ice right into the kitchen and deposit it into the icebox. He was a good-natured man who sang lustily as he drove along his route, and he allowed us to hop on back of the wagon and dangle our feet as we rode along with him for a block or two.

Patsy Allen lived around the corner, and we loved to play dress up. Many times we put on her mother's clothes, including high heel shoes, hats and gloves, and maybe even lipstick. Once when Dr. Allen returned home he tipped his hat and spoke to us so cordially that we thought he had mistaken us for grown-ups. He was a fun-loving person who entered into many happy adventures with Patsy and me, always appearing to have just as much fun as we did. He and Mrs. Allen were a warm, affectionate couple and all of my memories of being in their home are happy ones. Dr. Allen filled a void in my life because I did not remember my father, and I think they made a special effort to make me feel a part of their family.

MAMA'S OLDER SISTER, AUNT MABEL, was a registered nurse, spending most of her long career as Night Supervisor at Erlanger Hospital in Chattanooga, Tennessee. She always encouraged

Mama in her efforts to keep us together, and she generously shared what little she could spare from her limited income to help us, even though she also provided a large part of Grandma's support. Aunt Mabel never married and we were her only nieces and nephews. The major portion of our Christmas gifts came from her. She carefully selected appropriate books for each one of us, not only for Christmas but also for our birthdays. Two successful authors of children's books, Christine Noble Govan and her daughter, Emmy Payne, were also very close friends of Aunt Mabel. All of us children received books that were lovingly inscribed by Aunt Mabel and personally autographed by Mrs. Govan and Emmy. We still treasure those books today and have enjoyed sharing them with our children and grandchildren.

In addition to books, Aunt Mabel sent each one of us an article of clothing and one other Christmas gift. I still have a little purse shaped like a Scotty dog that she sent me on one occasion.

My favorite gift was a Shirley Temple doll, and its tragic end remains one of my saddest memories. It involves Billy Randolph, another neighbor, but he was not my friend. He and my oldest brother, Howard, were the same age, and I thought Billy was the meanest boy I ever knew. After Billy and Howard saw the picture show (that's what we called movies back then) *Marie Antoinette*, it inspired them to build a guillotine. They spent a lot of time drawing plans for it, finding scraps of wood to use, and taking apart a large kitchen knife in order to use the blade. Proud of the results of their effort, they decided to test it by beheading my Shirley Temple doll! I was heartbroken, and I still get mad when I think about it. They even buried her and never would tell me where her little grave was. Billy moved away from Auburn a few years later, and I heard that he eventually became a surgeon in the Miami area. I trust he had developed some compassion by then.

MRS. F. W. BURNS, WHO LIVED ACROSS the street and a few doors down, had a friend, Mrs. L. W. Spratling from Gold Hill, who frequently came to see her, bringing her little granddaughter, Miriam Ann Kirkwood, with her. Miriam Ann (when we said her name it sounded like "Maryman") is a year younger than I am, and we became great friends, playing together while Mrs. Burns and Mrs. Spratling visited.

Mrs. Kirkwood died of pneumonia when Miriam Ann was a baby, but I didn't know that at the time. I just knew that her mother was dead and that she lived with her grandparents, Dr. and Mrs. Spratling, who were very old, I thought. I realize now that they were probably younger than I am today, and I don't feel old at all.

Mrs. Spratling told Mama that Miriam Ann had no playmates because they lived so far out in the country, and she asked if I could spend a few days with them. That was the beginning of a long-lasting friendship and many happy visits in the Spratling home. A number of times Dr. Spratling, a tall, stately man and a retired Navy surgeon, would drive over those dirt (usually muddy) roads to pick me up, and I would visit in their beautiful home, Roamers' Roost, for several days until homesickness overcame me. The Spratlings had lots of servants who lived in little cabins on the place, something that I was not accustomed to. They had a cook, a maid who served our meals, two wash women who collected the soiled clothes and linens every morning, and I don't know how many men worked out in the fields. It was a wonderful place, and the Spratlings were dear, gentle people who made me feel welcome and loved.

Their home was huge and elegantly furnished, and they also had a bungalow on the grounds that Miriam Ann called the "playhouse." Actually it was a house with two or three bedrooms. It was not occupied at that time, so we used it for tea parties and playing dolls.

Most of all, I loved playing in the attic of the big house where there were trunks of clothes and beautiful articles from Japan where Dr. and Mrs. Spratling had gone on their wedding trip. We were allowed to play dress-up in the most exquisite dresses with shawls and gloves and hats. What a dream place for little girls to enjoy.

For some reason, I always thought that Miriam Ann's mother died in an upstairs bedroom opposite the stairway and next to the linen closet. Each time I passed that room I turned my head with a little shudder because I thought there just might be a ghost watching me. Only recently I learned that Mrs. Kirkwood actually died in the Opelika Hospital shortly after Miriam Ann's birth.

The huge linen closet had stacks and stacks of beautiful sheets and pillowcases, always starched and ironed, and it smelled heavenly. The towels were arranged in perfect order according to their color and the appropriate bathroom for each set.

At the time I didn't realize how fortunate I was to enjoy all the luxuries and kindnesses bestowed on me by Dr. and Mrs. Spratling, but even now, sixty years later, I can enjoy those memories with a wonderful sense of nostalgia. When I visit Miriam Ann's brother, Kenneth Spratling (Husky) Kirkwood and his wife, Alice, who now live at Roamers' Roost, I have many warm memories and a grand feeling of going back to my childhood.

OUR FIRST RADIO WAS A GIFT FROM DR. ANN SOMMER, a Soil Chemist in the Department of Agronomy and Soils.

She rented a room at the Grimes house next door and always seemed interested in our family. Many times she found ways to give us gifts or help Mama in ways that would not cause embarrassment. Dr. Sommer won a research award of $1,500 for discovering several minor elements in soil that were necessary for plant growth. She used part of her award to buy a new radio and record player for herself. When the workmen came to install the antenna (all radios required outside antennae then) she had them install the old antenna at our house and deliver the old radio to us. We were overjoyed and we watched for Mama to come home from work that afternoon. I remember racing to see who could get to her first with the exciting news about the radio.

Dr. Sommer had no close relatives, and I think the exuberance of our active family filled a void in her somewhat quiet and lonely life.

AUNT MABEL TOOK HER VACATIONS in August, and each year she would visit us on the way to Mississippi to see Grandma and Aunt Alma and Uncle Emory. She would arrive by train since she didn't have a car, and a week later would continue by train for the rest of her trip. Those were happy times, and we loved Aunt Mabel, as she did us. She had a Kodak camera that pulled out with an accordion type arrangement in front. She always took pictures of us, and I realize now that had she not done this we would have had very few pictures of us growing up. Mama was meticulous in dating and identifying each picture, most of them taken in August, of course.

Aunt Mabel was a wonderful person, devoted to her family and supportive of Mama in her struggles to keep us together. The photographs as well as our extensive collection of books were gifts that enriched our young lives and remain treasured possessions to this day.

One of the things I learned from Aunt Mabel was that it is all right to write in margins of books. She was a voracious reader and an avid collector of books, especially those having anything to do with history, religion, nature, and current events. She had numerous commentaries on the Bible, and she read and studied her Bible faithfully every day. When she was about eight years

37

old, she made a pledge at her Sunday School class that she would never let a day go by without reading her Bible, and I believe she lived up to that promise as long as she was able and her eyesight permitted. One of her books that she read over and over, *The Bible as History* by Werner Keller, has copious marginal notes as well as many newspaper clippings pasted in the front and back of the book. For example, one clipping, dated October 1963, reports that Turkish archaeologists have uncovered what they believe is a fresco portrait of the Greek philosopher Socrates in excavations at the ruins of Ephesus on the Aegean Coast. On page 347 is a description from ancient Chinese sources of Halley's Comet. Next to this paragraph she wrote in the margin, "May 13, 1910 [we were living in Thomas, Oklahoma, at the time] my stepfather sat up with me to see Halley's Comet which appeared around 1:30 a.m." Aunt Mabel was fourteen at the time and that exciting event remained a vivid memory as long as she lived.

I love reading books from Aunt Mabel's extensive library, and her clippings and comments make them even more interesting and informative.

Aunt Mabel had fallen off a high bed when she was a very young child, and I am convinced that she broke her nose and jaw in that fall. Her baby pictures, which were taken prior to that time, were as pretty as Mama's, but as an adult, with protruding teeth and a misshapen nose, she would have been described as homely. She was beautiful to me because I loved her so, and she was greatly admired by the many nurses who worked under her supervision, but I think that accident had a lasting effect on the course of her life. However, she was dedicated to her profession, and she never gave the impression that she had any regrets about her life. She told me once that the hospital and staff were her home and family.

She lived in Harriet Pearson Hall, a dormitory for nursing students at Erlanger Hospital in Chattanooga, Tennessee, from the time it was built in 1925 until 1977, when it was razed to make room for another building. It was a beautiful building with marble floors and interesting architectural details, and it saddened her to learn that it would be demolished. Since she had to vacate her apartment there, I suggested that she consider moving to Auburn. She was eighty-two years old at the time, and she and I both realized that she might need to be near her family. She lived here for thirteen years before her death in 1990, and they may have been the happiest years of her life.

Aunt Mabel had a lifelong interest in wildlife and she was especially interested in birds. She had been a member of the Chattanooga Ornithological Society and she often told of the interesting bird-watching trips she enjoyed with this group. Our former minister, Charles Britt, officiated at her funeral service. We were gathered under a tent at her graveside in Memorial Park Cemetery, and just as Charles told of her intense interest in birds and of her

bird-watching trips, a beautiful hummingbird flew under the tent. As we watched in astonishment, the tiny bird hovered over the grave, fluttered its wings for a moment, and then flew away, leaving us momentarily speechless. I think of that brief scene as Aunt Mabel's final farewell to her devoted family and friends.

Mama and Aunt Mabel Agnes Norman on Mabel's eighty-ninth birthday, August 27, 1984

39

Mama with Howard (standing) and Wesley and Norman (seated), August 1938

Four
The Methodist Children's Home

IN THE SUMMER OF 1937, MAMA WAS AT A POINT where she was desperate for relief from some of her burdens, not only financial needs but also the exhausting demands on her time. Our minister at that time was the Reverend Carleton Preer and Mama asked him for advice. He suggested that she consider sending the two oldest boys (Howard and Norman) to the Methodist Orphanage in Selma. At first she rejected this idea completely, feeling that there must be a better solution that would not require the separation of her children. She replied that her children were not orphans, and Brother Preer assured her that very few of the children at the orphanage had actually lost both parents. He told her that of the 154 children living there at that time only three were orphans. He went on to say, "This is a solution that is not permanent but should provide some temporary relief. It won't hurt the boys and they might find it a beneficial experience. At the end of the school year, the orphanage will be glad to release them back to you, you will be happy to have them home again, and the boys will be thrilled to come back home."

WHEN I BECAME AN ADULT, I DISCOVERED that there had been a very strong possibility that we could have been orphans when Daddy died. When Norman was born on December 11, 1924, in the parsonage at Stockton, Alabama, Mama almost hemorrhaged to death, and her physician, Dr. John H. Hastie, told Daddy then that another pregnancy might be fatal for her. For that reason, when it was time for Wesley's birth in April 1927, Daddy decided that Mama should be hospitalized for the delivery. They were living in Marion Junction and they rushed to Selma, fifteen miles away, where Wesley was born in Vaughn Memorial Hospital. So Wes has the distinction of being the only one of the six children who was born in a hospital.

When I was born April 25, 1929, in the parsonage at Pine Apple, Alabama, Dr. Erskine Donald was extremely apprehensive about Mama's health and he advised Daddy that there should be no more babies. Two years later when Lamar, the youngest child, was born, Dr. Donald was gravely concerned about Mama and he feared that she would not survive Lamar's birth. Dr. Donald was so afraid that Mama would not live through the night that he told Daddy to bring each of the children to her bedside to tell her goodbye. Wesley vividly remembers holding Daddy's hand as he was led into the darkened room, seeing Mama with her newborn baby girl and leaving the room, crying softly. He was four years old, and at that young age this poignant event became his earliest memory.

THE DECISION TO SEND HOWARD AND NORMAN to the Children's Home was an exceedingly difficult one for Mama to make, and I know there were times in later years when she reflected on it and wondered if it was the right thing to do. Howard was fourteen and Norman was twelve at the time. They came home for holidays, and Mama wrote them frequently. She would have done everything in her power to keep them from feeling abandoned or rejected.

Some of our family friends lived in Selma or nearby, and Norman remembers that they were attentive, taking the boys to their homes for weekend visits. The Caleys would pick them up on Fridays and sometimes they would ride with either Mrs. Caley or Mabel to deliver eggs to one or more grocery stores in Selma before going to Marion Junction for the weekend. Norman remembers at least one weekend with the Farishes in Orrville, and the Jackson family in Selma invited them to their home for frequent visits.

When the boys came home for Thanksgiving holidays Howard spent most of his time working on his old bicycle. He wanted it with him in Selma so that he could enjoy it for the rest of the school year. He decided that it would be exciting to ride it at least part of the way, and he knew he better have it in the best possible shape in order to get Mama's permission. He was an adventurous sort anyway, and this was a thrilling way to transport his bike to Selma. Wesley remembers riding with Charlie Mack Stokes in a pickup truck to the other side of Montgomery, and watching Howard unload his bike at the top of a long hill where he took off pedaling toward Selma—about fifty miles away. Howard always thought of that as a great expedition, and he was exhilarated by it. Mama had agreed to it reluctantly and with many misgivings.

My brothers returned home in the summer of 1938, and Brother Preer's prediction was correct. We were thrilled to have them home again and they were just as happy to be back with their family.

A LATER MINISTER OF THE AUBURN METHODIST CHURCH was not as compassionate or supportive of Mama's efforts as Brother Preer had been. I will refer to him as Dr. W.

Each year in September Mama borrowed $100 from the Bank of Auburn in order to buy school books and pay for other necessary expenses for us to begin the school year. She had always gotten her annual widow's pension from the Alabama Methodist Conference in October and it was slightly more than $100— usually $110. This was the only payment she received each year and she counted on that check to repay the bank loan. Imagine her dismay when the check came in October 1941 in the amount of $45.08. She went to see Dr. W. to find out if he knew anything about it, and he told her, somewhat smugly, that he had reported to Annual Conference that they should reduce Mrs. Ellis's pension check because "her children were dressed as well as any other children in the church."

In disbelief that he could have done something so heartless without at least saying something to her beforehand, she replied, "But Dr. W., the reason my children are dressed as well as they are is because most of their clothes are hand-me-downs from compassionate and generous friends. All the others I make myself, and many of those are made from fabric that has been given to me." He made no apology and the following year her check was $44.59. Mama appealed to the Presiding Elder, Dr. D. P. Slaughter, a longtime friend who had officiated at Daddy's funeral. He saw to it that her pension was increased and by 1945 the check she received was $121.03.

MY BROTHER WESLEY ALSO SPENT A SCHOOL YEAR away from Auburn, and I asked him to record his memories of that time. The following is his account:

> In the summer of 1935, we were living on South Gay Street in Auburn. It was a wonderful neighborhood with playmates living in practically every house from Samford Avenue to Thach Avenue, a distance of about two blocks. Next door was the Grimes family with daughters Betty and Mary Frances, who are still close friends after more than sixty years. Two doors up the street was the Lowery family, and

continuing up and down on either side of the street were the Tidmores, the Sims, the Burns, the Reeves, the Wrights, the Hills, the Hares, the Tisdales, the Wares, and the Williamsons. These families all had children who became our playmates, and we still count them as our friends.

The Homer Wright family lived a half block from us, and Mr. Wright's sister, Barbara, was married to Mr. E. C. Easter (called Pap by his friends), an executive with Alabama Power Company in Birmingham. The Easters had only one child, Everett, Jr., who was called Bubba by his family and friends. Bubba was six months younger than I, but we were in the same grade at school.

Mrs. Easter was unable to have more children and Everett, as I remember it, had had some health problems. The Easters felt that if he had a live-in playmate or companion—a surrogate brother—it would be a big help in his emotional development. They discussed this with the Wrights, asking if they knew of a suitable candidate. They immediately thought of the large family that had recently moved down the street with a son about the same age as Everett. Mr. and Mrs. Wright knew, of course, the difficult task that Mama had ahead of her, and they probably felt that such an arrangement could be beneficial to both families. They discussed it with Mama and she, in turn, talked to me.

The scene is firmly implanted in my memory. Mama was giving me a bath, and she told me of a little boy who had no brothers or sisters. Being in the middle of six children, that very idea of being an only child was probably inconceivable to me at the time. Mama asked me if I would like to be his playmate and live in Birmingham for the school year. I think I readily agreed, although I do not remember my exact response. I do remember, however, that I never felt that I was being rejected or abandoned, and I don't remember being homesick during the year in Birmingham. I was born with wanderlust and viewed the move to Birmingham as an exciting travel adventure.

Certainly, the year I spent in Birmingham provided me with opportunities that I would not have had otherwise. I think there is no doubt that my lifelong involvement with music has its roots in that year of my life. Musically, the high point of the year was my introduction to the world of opera. The Birmingham Opera Company presented, on April 30, 1936, Bizet's *Carmen*. There was an afternoon matinee for the public schools, and I was enthralled by the entire experience. I had not known there was such a thing. In the vernacular of the present-day, younger generation, I was completely blown away with my first opera.

Miss Sue Finklea was my music teacher at Avondale School, and she had done a thorough job of preparing her young charges for the performance. Her telling of the story was so vivid and exciting that I remember the plot sixty-five years later, and I have never re-read the libretto. There were a couple of incredible coincidences which arose from my childhood association with *Carmen*. First, Sue Finklea stands out in my memory as the teacher I remember most affectionately from that year in Birmingham. In fact, she is the only one I remember. I adored her and thought she was the prettiest teacher I had ever seen. In 1950, when I moved to Mobile, Alabama, to take my first teaching job at Murphy High School, Sue Finklea, by then Mrs. Sue Finklea Morgan, was teaching in the Mobile School System. We renewed our friendship and had many pleasant contacts which continued even after I left the teaching field.

The second, and even more amazing, coincidence involved Josephine Wehby Sharbel, a well-known soprano in Birmingham, who sang the role of Frasquita in the performance of

Carmen which I attended. Fifty-five years later on June 15, 1991, her grandson, Arthur John (Buddy) Sharbel III, married my daughter, Leslie, at St. Elias Church in Birmingham. What a small world we live in.

I don't know how beneficial my year with the Easters proved to be for Everett, but it added an important dimension to my life, and I will always remember the Easter family with affection and gratitude.

Wesley's interest in music deepened after he returned to Auburn, and the narrative of his involvement in the world of music should be continued in his words.

I began the study of piano at age ten with Mrs. Arvey Carnes, whose husband was head of the Agricultural Engineering Department at A.P.I., and, therefore, Mama's boss. Mrs. Carnes must have been a wonderful teacher because I remember eagerly anticipating every lesson. I learned rapidly, and after only a year of piano, I began playing for the Sunday School at the First Baptist Church in Auburn. We were Methodists, but back then we went wherever our friends went. I can remember going to the Baptist Sunday School, to the Methodist Church, and to the Presbyterian Youth Group (Christian Endeavor, I think it was called) on Sunday evenings. We gained quite an ecumenical foundation in religion.

At the Baptist Sunday School, Mrs. Grimes, our next-door neighbor, was the department head. Truly one of the dearest women in the world, Mrs. Grimes had a commanding, austere manner which inspired absolute obedience (and probably a little fright) in the children of the neighborhood. Although I was devoted to her, I was also terrified of her.

I credit Mrs. Grimes, who did not read music, with my ability to sight-read music. One Sunday, when she announced the next hymn, I turned to the proper page and my heart sank. It was "When They Ring Those Golden Bells," which has a dotted-eighth/sixteenth-note rhythm—a difficult rhythmic pattern for a small child with only one year of piano lessons. With a feeling of terror, I turned to Mrs. Grimes and said desperately, "Oh, Mrs. Grimes, I can't play this one."

She looked at me and said sternly, "Yes, you can." And I did. I was afraid not to. I never told her again that I couldn't play a hymn.

Any pianist knows that the key to learning to sight-read is to jump in, plow through it, and never, ever stop. This forces you to read ahead and, at the same time, trains you to read faster and faster, becoming a good sight-reader. This ability is an invaluable tool for musicians and particularly for church musicians. It has always been one of my strengths, and I give Mrs. Grimes full credit for helping (or perhaps forcing) me to develop this gift.

Five
Another Move

Mr. B. C. Pope, who owned the house we lived in, sold it in 1937 and we had to move. Mrs. Grimes was so distressed over our having to move that she made every effort to find us another place in the neighborhood, but there was nothing available.

The only house Mama found that she could afford to rent was at 142 Donahue Drive, and the rent was $15 a month. It was a small frame house, four rooms with a sleeping porch, and a bathroom, once again, at the end of the back porch. There was a pasture that we shared with three other families and each family had a cow. My brothers had to take turns milking our cow, Princess. That was a chore which caused much grumbling, but we always had plenty of milk and butter. The butter had to be churned, and we took turns doing that. A special treat was when Mama made pull candy and we had great fun pulling the long ropes of buttery candy until it was smooth and golden yellow, and then we cut the rope into bite-size pieces. It stuck to our teeth, but it tasted delicious.

The pasture and the houses surrounding it belonged to Mrs. Bernard Cowart*, widow of an A.P.I. professor who had bought large tracts of land in and around Auburn. He had built a number of rental houses on his land, so the Cowart family was probably one of the wealthiest families in Auburn. We didn't want to move to that little house, a long way from our friends and almost two miles from school. However, that move precipitated events years later which changed Mama's life—exciting and positive changes, though the realization of them created a great deal of stress and anxiety.

The water heater was attached to the woodburning stove in the bathroom, and on cold winter mornings that was the only room that was warm. Water ran through coils inside the stove and when it came out of a tap on the other side, it was nicely heated. There was also a woodburning cook stove in the kitchen, and many times when we got home from school in the afternoon we would get leftover biscuits from the warming ovens at the top of the stove, punch a hole in the side of the biscuit and pour it full of thick brown ribbon cane syrup. It was pretty messy, but a great snack. We had lots of fresh vegetables from our garden in the summer, and Mama canned as many as possible to use during the winter months. I still remember the delicious special taste of cornbread as well as biscuits baked in the oven of a woodburning stove. We cooked our vegetables with fat back, and a favorite treat was to cut open a cornbread muffin, spoon blackeyed peas over it, and drown it in pot likker. A bowl of grits on the side with sliced tomatoes from the garden made a delicious supper. We had supper in the evenings, and dinner was a big noontime meal—usually on Sundays. We rarely had meat except on Sunday. Many times we had the same menu day after day, depending on what was available and cheap, but we never went to bed hungry.

Books have always been important in our lives, and I am grateful to Mama and to Aunt Mabel for encouraging us to discover the joys of reading. Mama had us read a chapter or two of classic books each night after supper. Usually Mama and the older children would take turns reading a paragraph. It was an exciting day when each of us younger ones learned to read well enough to take a turn. Maybe we didn't always read that well, because I remember the older ones indicating their impatience by sighing and groaning as a first or second grader struggled with the words in *Little Women, Tom Sawyer,* or *Treasure Island.*

Mama and Daddy had both been accustomed to family prayers in their own families and had continued the practice in ours. Mama carried on this tradition after Daddy's death, and a short period every evening before bedtime was set aside for prayers. We sat in a circle while the older children took turns reading a scripture lesson, and then Mama led us in prayer—each of us adding a sentence or two. Sometimes these had to do with happenings of the day—sometimes with anticipated problems, like a test the following day—many times we added a memorized sentence which is probably what Lamar and I said until we grew older and more creative. Once I peeped and saw Wesley had his eyes open which I reported to Mama. I never tattled about that again because she pointed out that I had to have my eyes open in order to know that Wesley's were too.

Life went on in our little house on Donahue Drive, the days, then years slipping by.

Like most little pre-teen girls, my friends and I thought spend-the-night parties were the best. I had these occasionally at our house but we usually went to Gene Hurt's or Shay Tidmore's or Patsy Allen's or Yvonne Cargile's. They lived in beautiful brick houses, and the Tidmores even had two bathrooms, an unheard-of luxury in those days. I am ashamed to confess it now, but I was embarrassed because, instead of blankets, we had quilts made by my grandmother, and we usually had homemade biscuits instead of toast. How our priorities change. Now I consider it a

51

*Mama with Carolyn
and Lamar, August
1938*

luxury to use those beautiful quilts and to wake up to the smell
of homemade biscuits.

Helen Edwards lived in the country, and her house was a favorite place to have spend-the-night parties because they had a
lake, there were horses that we could ride, and Mrs. Edwards was
a wonderful cook. Or maybe the cooking was done by their maid,
Caldonia. We loved to call out her name in loud voices and then
sing the first line of the song, "Caldonia, What make yo' big
head so hard? " To get it just right, you had to sing Cal-**don**-yuh,
coming down hard on the second syllable and sliding up about
an octave higher on the last one. She pretended to be upset with
us, but I think she loved the attention.

One night when we went to Helen's, we were thrilled to see
that Mrs. Hurt (Gene's mother) had made one of her famous
three-layer devil's food cakes with seven-minute icing for our

midnight snack. The mountains of white icing swirls made our mouths water in anticipation every time we looked at that cake, but we had to wait because Dr. Edwards hadn't gotten home yet and Mrs. Edwards never served dinner until he arrived, regardless of the time. Finally our dinner was served and we raced through the meal.

It must have been almost midnight when we finished eating, and we hurriedly got ready for bed and climbed into the bunk beds on the back porch. There were two sets of double-decker beds, and the cake was placed on the floor between them. For some reason, it seemed important for us to wait until midnight for our midnight snack. Maybe it was because we had never stayed up that late before. Anyway, someone threw a rubber frog in one of the top bunks and Jane Keener jumped out like she'd been shot. When she hit the floor one foot landed right smack in the middle of that cake! We all looked in dismay at the white and chocolate footprint, with cake squashed out on the floor all around it. Then someone observed that the cake outside of the footprint would be fine to eat, just a little messy. That seemed like a reasonable solution, so we got spoons and ate all around the footprint, getting closer and closer to it. Before the night was over every crumb of the cake had been eaten, footprint and all.

SINCE MAMA WORKED SUCH LONG HOURS and could not be there when we got home from school each day, we had a servant, Bessie Atkinson. She came early in the morning, fixed breakfast, and got us off to school. Then she washed clothes in a washpot outside, and hung them out to dry. She did the ironing and straightened up the house before walking back to her little house a few blocks away. She returned just before time for us to get home from school and cooked supper. Bessie did all of this for $2.50 a week "plus totes." That meant that she ate what we ate, but she always toted leftovers home in a syrup

53

bucket to feed her pig. I don't think her pig was very fat because there were few leftovers at our house.

Each of us had to make our beds, hang up our clothes, and keep our communal rooms neat. Mama had little time for housework other than sewing in the evenings. However, she usually fixed Sunday morning breakfast and we had toast instead of our usual biscuits. We had no pop-up toaster back then so the toast was browned in the oven of our wood-burning stove. Of course, it didn't have a thermostat and Mama invariably burned at least one pan of toast. Our oldest brother, Howard, never missing an opportunity to tease, would sniff dramatically and as soon as he smelled smoke he would say in a loud voice that Mama would be sure to hear, "It must be Sunday. I smell toast burning."

When I was about ten years old, one of my most vivid childhood memories occurred during a severe thunderstorm. I've always been exhilarated by storms, and I liked to stand at our back door, looking out over the pasture when dark clouds started forming and the rumble of thunder could be heard. One summer day Norman and I were standing at the back door, knowing that a severe storm was approaching. We watched the neighborhood cows crowding under a large tree in the middle of the pasture. Each of the four families who rented the houses around the pasture kept a cow. We had a black Jersey named Princess and our next-door neighbor, Mrs. Bessie Bailey (whose son Wilford later became President of Auburn University), had a large milk cow, a Guernsey I think. The other families had cows, too, but I don't remember them. Norman and I will never forget Mrs. Bailey's cow because she was struck by lightning as we watched her. Her huge body went straight up in the air, several feet at least, and when she fell back to the ground, she was dead.

I have wondered how that body was disposed of, but I don't think I stayed to watch it. More than thirty years later our son, James, decided that our horse needed a greener pasture and more

Carolyn, 1940

grass for grazing. James was about ten years old then, and he rode out to George and Dorry Johnston's farm to see if he could leave Flash there to graze for a few weeks. George very generously agreed for him to leave the horse. The next Sunday, while we were having Sunday dinner, George called and told my husband some sad news. During a severe thunderstorm, lightening had struck and killed Flash. Lan asked, "What in thunder do you do with a dead horse?" and George told him that Jack and Margie Bailey were having lunch with them and that Jack said he could take care of the horse. Jack was in the construction business and his backhoe driver could dig a hole next to the horse, push it over into the hole, and cover it up. This sounded like a wonderful solution to a terrible problem, so Lan was happy to have Jack take care of it.

The backhoe driver was called Snake because he was a very tall, very thin black man. He took the backhoe out to the Johnston farm the next morning and took care of Flash's burial. Lan had bought that horse at an auction in Phenix City for $75, and he loved to tell the story about his $75 horse which was buried by a man called Snake at a cost of $125. Our children, grief-stricken over their beloved horse, would not have thought that was the least bit funny, so Lan was careful not to tell it in their presence.

Six
School Days

In the May 25, 1939, issue of *The Alabama Christian Advocate,* a publication of the Methodist Church, the following article appeared:

> Here is a record of scholarship achievement rarely,
> if ever, attained by the children in one family in the State of
> Alabama. Lamar Ellis, a little girl named for the late Dr. A. J.
> Lamar*, made the highest record in the second grade; Caro-
> lyn Ellis, a sister, made the highest record in the fourth grade;
> Wesley Ellis, a brother, made the highest record in the sixth
> grade; Norman Ellis, an older brother, made the highest
> record in the eighth grade; and Gay Ellis, the oldest sister,
> was recently chosen the D.A.R. Good Citizenship Girl of the
> Senior Class in high school and will be awarded the medal
> for scholarship at the commencement, May 26, 1939. All of
> this occurred in the schools at Auburn, Alabama, and these
> are the children of Mrs. H. M. Ellis and the late Rev. H. M.

---

*Before their sixth and last baby was born, Daddy expressed a wish to name the child, boy or girl, for his close friend and fellow Methodist preacher, Dr. Andrew Jackson Lamar.

Ellis, who was for some years a member of the Alabama Conference. Not only the people of Eutaw, Brother Ellis' last pastorate, but many other friends throughout the state will be happy to know of the unusually fine record made by these children of a noble father and a consecrated mother. To the proud mother and all the children we offer our hearty congratulations and pray God's continued blessings upon them all as they carry on toward ever-enlarging achievements.

Mama was exceedingly proud of our scores on the Achievement Tests that year, and later ones too, but she worried because Howard was the only one who did not excel in his studies. He had rheumatic fever when he was in the third grade and missed a lot of school. In addition, he had had a very poor first-grade teacher. To make matters worse, Howard had chronic ear infections which affected his hearing. So his schooling got off to a bad start, through no fault of his own, and although he was just as smart as the rest of us, he was "not scholarly" as he so aptly put it. He had a wonderful sense of humor and wrote priceless letters that we all treasure.

Howard and Norman both played football in high school, and that was when Mama became one of Auburn's biggest football fans, a passion which endured even when she could no longer go to the games. Howard had a stocky build, and he played guard on the Lee County High School team. We didn't become a city school system, changing the name to Auburn High School, until around 1960. Howard was a first string guard, but he didn't get the spotlight as he would have had he been in the backfield, until one glorious moment when he intercepted a pass and ran for a touchdown. After that Mama almost never missed a high school or college game, and during her long years of retirement she watched many of the professional games on television.

She frequently wrote to the coaches—high school, college, and professional—sometimes to praise them, but many times to tell them of mistakes that she thought they had made. It was amazing how many of those coaches responded. Maybe it was because she always started out by revealing her age—eighty, eighty-five, ninety years old—whatever it happened to be at the time. She wrote a blistering letter to Coach Woody Hayes of Ohio State concerning his remarks about our team after Auburn University was named National Champions in 1957. She did not get a response to that letter, and I'm glad. I think Coach Hayes could have written a letter that matched hers and more.

She wrote Coach Barry Switzer of Oklahoma a letter and received a cordial reply from him. It must have been after we lost to Oklahoma in the Sugar Bowl in 1972. Her letter probably was courteous and complimentary. Mama always had a special feeling for Oklahoma since that was her birthplace. However, her feelings did not extend to a desire for them to win if they were playing Auburn.

At an Auburn-Mississippi State game in Jackson, the M.S.U. cheerleaders turned the amplifiers in such a way that the ringing of the cowbells in their cheering section was deafening to those of us sitting on the other side of the field. Mama was listening to the game at home, and she was distracted by the noise in the background. As it increased in volume she became furious at what she considered to be unsportsmanlike behavior. She conveyed her feelings in letters to the Mississippi State coach, Charlie Shira, as well as their athletic director and their president. She told them that she had always been a fan of Mississippi State and that she pulled for them against every team they played except when they played Auburn. She added that she was disappointed that they would have allowed such a thing to happen. Each of these men responded in a courteous manner, and that restored some of her feelings for Mississippi State. Later when her grandson

Bill Smyer joined their faculty she forgot any feelings of hostility that might have lingered.

Mama also wrote to players to commend them for jobs well done. If they made spectacular plays that may have determined the outcome of a game, she went a step further and made a pillow commemorating a particular play or game. The Auburn-Alabama game on December 2, 1972, at Legion Field in Birmingham will always be remembered as one of the greatest in the history of Auburn football. Auburn fans will recall that this is the game fondly called Punt-Bama-Punt. There was a spirit and determination to win displayed by our team that cannot be forgotten, and the entire team deserves credit for the remarkable victory that day. If heroes were singled out they would have to be Bill Newton, Roger Mitchell, Gardner Jett, David Langner, and Dave Beck. The first three—Newton, Mitchell, and Jett—came to Auburn as walk-ons. Langner and Beck had scholarships, but because of their size they were considered marginal. They proved themselves to be giants that day.

Alabama scored its first touchdown in the second quarter, and Mitchell blocked the extra point. As David Housel put it in *Saturdays to Remember,* "Never would one point turn out to mean so much." A field goal just before the end of the first half put Alabama ahead 9-0. To make matters worse, Auburn had only eight yards offense.

Alabama was on a roll, and although their fans were making a thunderous noise from the west side of the field, the Auburn fans had not given up on their team. At the end of the third quarter the score was Alabama 16-0. But, oh, what glories were in store for us. With 9:50 left to play in the game, Auburn finally got on the scoreboard when Gardner Jett kicked a 42-yard field goal, the longest he had ever kicked. My husband, Lan, and I were there, and somehow we knew that the game was far from over. When Alabama's Gantt attempted a punt on fourth down,

Bill Newton blocked his kick. David Langner got to the ball on the 25 yard line and raced into the end zone. Dave Beck got a wobbly snap from center, but put it squarely on the tee, and Jett's kick made it 16-10. With just over five minutes left on the clock, Auburn kicked off and Alabama ground out three first downs. On the next series they were four yards short of a first down, and Mike Neel stopped Davis for a four-yard loss. Alabama would have to punt, and I turned to Lan and said, "You know, this could happen again!" Miracle of miracles—Newton blocked the kick, and just as if they had had a dress rehearsal, Langner fielded the ball, this time running it in from the 20. All eyes were again on Gardner Jett and he *did* it. He scored the extra point and the scoreboard flashed Auburn 17, Alabama 16. With little over a minute left to play, Alabama made one first down, and then on second down their quarterback passed. David Langner (who else?) was waiting to intercept it on the 42.

Pandemonium reigned and Auburn people everywhere were celebrating. PUNT, BAMA, PUNT! and 17-16 bumper stickers, reminders of the miracle at Legion Field, started appearing on cars within minutes it seemed of Auburn's victory.

Mama watched every minute of that game on television and remembered just about every play. She took our three youngest children, Lan, James, and Katherine, to Toomer's Corner to take part in the huge celebration and the tossing of hundreds of rolls of toilet paper in the trees and power lines there. Later she made sure that she and our children were on hand to welcome our team home from their victorious trip. The next day she read all the sports sections, not just the Birmingham and Opelika-Auburn papers, which she read every day anyway, but she went out and bought the Montgomery and Atlanta papers, too.

She immediately started planning the orange and blue pillows that she would embroider with tigers and eagles (Auburn's mascots), the date and score, and the name of the person for whom she made it. These handmade pillows were her way of showing her heroes that she thought they were great. I don't know how many of these she made, but I do remember that she was worried about all of the attention that Newton and Langner were getting, certainly well-deserved. But, as she pointed out, "What if Gardner Jett had missed one of his kicks?" I know that she made one of the pillows for him, and I also remember that she received not only a thank-you note from Gardner, but also a lovely letter from his mother.

All of Mama's grandchildren who are Auburn fans were also blessed with one of her special pillows. I have one that is threadbare and well-loved, but it will never be thrown away.

ONE OF THE MOST EXCITING EVENTS DURING my teenage years was the day we got a telephone. Our number was 226-J, the letter at the end indicating that we were on a party line. Whoever shared that line with us must have gotten very exasperated because all of us children literally stood in line, waiting our turns to place calls. However, the neighbors who had so generously let us use their phones were probably relieved that the Ellis children from then on had their own. I especially remember Mrs. Nixon, who was always so beautiful and gracious, allowing us to make calls from their home. The Nixons' son, Billy, was a close friend of Norman and Wesley, and we used to spend many hours with him looking for golf balls on the old golf course which was on the west side of Wire Road and south of West Magnolia Avenue. We all grieved over Billy's tragic suicide when he was only nineteen, and even now, more than fifty years later, we think of him with longing and affection.

There was little privacy in our home, so I devised a secret signal for my friends and me to use while talking on the phone. If one of my siblings appeared to be eavesdropping while I was sharing secrets, I would use a sentence using the word "three" or "third." If I abruptly said something like, "She was sitting on the third row," then Gene, Shay, Patsy, Helen, Jane, Yvonne, or whomever I was talking to would know to change the subject. We thought that was such a clever scheme that we continued to use it for many years.

MAMA ALWAYS SAID THAT BESSIE ATKINSON literally came to work for us out of a cornfield. She had never worked in anyone's home before, and maybe that was just as well. Our little house with Mama and six children was not exactly typical, and Bessie learned to cook, wash and iron, and keep the house reasonably clean according to Mama's instructions. One of the most difficult things she had to learn was how to answer that telephone. She had never seen one before and she held it at arm's length as if she thought it might bite her. Actually it took a while for her to even get up the nerve to pick the durn thing up. If Mama called from work, she would hear the click when it was picked up, but then there was a dead silence. She could picture Bessie standing there, terror-stricken and her hands shaking. Mama would yell, "Bessie, answer the phone!" and finally she would hear a trembling "Hallo." Then when Mama would tell Bessie whatever it was that she had called about, she would hear the click of the phone being hung up. It was frustrating from Mama's end of the conversation, but when she got home she would see that Bessie had heard her and had carried out her instructions. Mama developed the same habit in her later years: that of hanging up without notice when she was finished with the business of her call.

Months later Bessie warmed up to the telephone and was finally able to use it comfortably. She even learned to place a call if necessary, picking up the phone and giving the operator Mama's number at work. Those calls were to be made only in the event of an emergency. Bessie's idea of what constituted an emergency didn't necessarily agree with Mama's, like calling to report that

63

Howard and Norman were having a fight or that one of the little ones had talked back to her. It was such an achievement for Bessie to make these calls that Mama didn't discourage her, but she did see to it that the calls were brief and to the point.

Bessie loved us and we loved her. One morning she reported that her daughter, Fannie Kate, had given birth to a baby girl the night before. Fannie Kate was only fifteen years old, and Bessie was the proud grandmother at twenty-nine. She reported that the baby's name was Elmer, and I said, "But I thought you said it was a girl, and Elmer is a boy's name." Bessie replied, "Is?" She never wasted words. I suggested that Evelyn would be a pretty name and that Elmer could be saved if she later had a boy. She and Fannie Kate liked that idea, and Evelyn is now a "settled lady" of about sixty. I don't think she ever knew how close she came to being named Elmer.

Bessie couldn't read and write, but she did learn her numbers if they were written in large print. She didn't have to read to be able to make the best biscuits in the world. When I failed miserably to copy her biscuits, Mama would say, "If Bessie can come in out of a cornfield and make biscuits, I know anyone with your intelligence can learn too." For once, Mama was wrong.

MAMA'S JOB AS SECRETARY TO DEAN FUNCHESS not only put her in touch with the faculty of the School of Agriculture but also with the staffs of the Agricultural Experiment Stations throughout Alabama. One time the director of the Chilton County Experiment Station brought big baskets of peaches to be shared by the staff in the dean's office. Mama decided to use most of hers to make pickled peaches, so on Saturday morning she showed Bessie how they should be peeled. When Mama got home from work at noon, she started right in with the job of preparing and putting up the peaches in quart jars. It was a hot summer day, and I can still remember how we were each assigned a task to make the job go faster, and what a relief it was when the last jar was sealed and placed on the pantry shelf. I probably wouldn't have remembered that if there hadn't been a sequel to the story.

After Bessie finished with the peaches, she hid the peelings in a big pot at the back of the cabinet under the sink. The next week she made peach brandy with those peelings, continuing to keep it hidden away. We began to detect a strong, pungent odor, and in a little while Howard and Norman discovered the source of it. They teased Bessie unmercifully and threatened to tell Mama if she didn't let them try it out first. I'm not sure that they tasted it, but I would be surprised if they didn't. I remember that they gave some to a little bantam chicken that Howard was raising. That chicken tried to get up and run away, and its legs would wobble and spread out like it was doing a split. They thought that was so funny that their next victim was a cat. (There were always a lot of stray animals that took up with us, and they must have been strong and persevering because they were often the brunt of my brothers' practical jokes.) The cat staggered around in circles for a little while and then slumped in a heap. I thought she was dead, but she slept off her indiscretions and when she revived she appeared to be unharmed by the escapade.

One time Howard and Norman caught a mouse, and they built a little glider plane out of heavy cardboard, just big enough to transport the unsuspecting victim on its first, and probably last, flight. They designed the plane with a trap door so the mouse could escape if he panicked. Then they attached a large handkerchief to the glider, securing each of the four corners so that it looked like a parachute. They climbed up in their tree house to launch the plane out over the pasture, but it didn't sail very far. When it hit the ground, the poor little mouse scurried out of the trap door and disappeared, apparently unhurt by the adventure.

THE TREE HOUSE WAS DESIGNED AND CONSTRUCTED by my brothers and was the site of many hours of play by our family as well as our friends. It served as our hiding place, a clubhouse, and a retreat. One of my older siblings, probably Howard, discovered that the handles on the fans at church were made of cross-vine and could be smoked just like a cigarette. Soon after that many of the fans in the balcony of the Auburn Methodist Church were missing handles, and I know where a lot of them went. Hidden away in the tree house, we tried smoking those handles, and I remember feeling dizzy and like my tongue was on fire. It was not exciting or fun in the least, and I was terrified that Mama would find out about our escapade.

Our tree house had to come down soon after that because Mr. Hurt, my friend Gene's father, happened to drive by and notice that the structure was perilously close to a live wire. Mr. Hurt was head of the Alabama Power Company in Auburn, and Mama was grateful that he made her aware of the potential danger. She lost no time in making sure that we abandoned the house and the tree it was lodged in.

Seven
Music

MAMA WAS A FIRM BELIEVER IN "PAYING AS YOU GO." If she couldn't pay cash for something then we did without. There was only one exception to this. She bought a piano from the Lewis Kerr family for $50, paying $5 down and then $5 a month until it was paid for. Mama had always regretted that she did not have the opportunity to take music lessons, and she was determined to give her children that chance. I don't know how much training Daddy had, but he played the piano and sang. Caroline Marshall Draughon, beloved wife of Auburn University President Ralph Brown Draughon, grew up in Orrville and knew my parents when Daddy served the Methodist Church there. She is one of the few people in Auburn who knew my father. She said that he had a beautiful voice and that she heard him sing in the Orrville Methodist Church many times. Mabel Caley Kelley Carlton still has fond memories of Daddy, especially of his singing *His Eye Is on the Sparrow.* In some of his smaller churches Daddy was choir director, pianist, and preacher. He even designed and built furniture for children's Sunday School rooms, and some of it is still in use in Marion Junction, more than seventy years later.

Gay and Wesley took piano lessons from Mrs. Arvey Carnes until she moved away, and then they took from Mrs. Iverson Caldwell. Later I started taking from Mrs. Caldwell and a couple of years later Lamar began. But Wesley is by far the most accomplished musician in our family. Mama had a rule that whoever was practicing after supper would be excused from washing dishes, and I think Wesley ate faster so he could beat us girls to the piano. He is also the most talented and motivated. After a year or so, Mrs. Caldwell did not charge anything for Wesley's lessons because, as she said, "He is the best advertisement I have." He played Liszt's *Hungarian Rhapsody, No. 2* for his last high school recital. The applause was thunderous and Mrs. Caldwell almost fainted with excitement. It was the first, and maybe the only, time that anyone ever played an encore at one of her recitals.

Mama not only sacrificed for us to have music lessons, but she also made sure that we attended the concerts presented on the A.P.I. campus. Each year she bought season tickets for all seven of us. We were never late for the performances either, and sometimes so early that the cleaning crew would still be pushing their brooms and straightening out the chairs. Nevertheless, Mama marched us right up to the front row so that we would not miss a thing; perhaps she also felt that we would behave better if we were right in front of the performers. When Gay, Howard, and Norman became teenagers they convinced Mama that they were old enough to sit a few rows back. Wesley, Lamar, and I were usually so spellbound by the performances that we sat in rapt attention. We especially remember hearing the Cincinnati Symphony at least two times, maybe more than that. Other memories are of hearing Blanche Thebom, mezzo soprano; Alexander Kipnis, Russian bass; Henry Cowell, composer and pianist; Gregor Piatagorsky, cellist; Carl Sandburg, poet; Robert Frost, poet; Ruggiero Ricci, violinist; Pearl Buck, author; and the original Trapp Family Singers.

The most unforgettable concert for me was Serge Jaroff conducting the Don Cossack Chorus and Dancers, November 23, 1939—when I was ten years old. These men, former officers of the Czar's Imperial Army, had organized their singing and dancing troup while in prison camp near Constantinople. They were exiled forever, with "en voyage" written in their League of Nations Nansen passports, and they poured into song all their hopeless longing for their homeland. A caption in the concert program read, "A Don Cossack concert is a thrilling experience. The exultant fervor of their voices in Russian sacred music, the passionate longing expressed in their folk songs, and the riotous accompaniment of shouts, whistling, and frenzied dancing in their Cossack war songs make a program that, once heard, is never forgotten."

I loved their music and dancing, but there is another reason that I will never forget those men—and one in particular. The following article, which appeared in the A.P.I. campus newspaper, *The Plainsman,* tells the story better than I can. It was written by Redding S. Sugg, Jr., a friend and neighbor who later had a distinguished career as an English professor, lecturer, and author:

> Last fall a little girl was sitting on the front row for the concert given by the Cossack Chorus and her mother and older sister were sitting behind her. The older sister soon became uncomfortable under the steady stare of a blond tenor who took solo parts, but shortly she noticed that his attention had been transferred to her little sister. During the rest of the concert the mother and older sister were aware that the tenor was intently watching the child, who at the close of the program turned to ask if she might ask an autograph of the man she liked best rather than of the leader. As if by mutual attraction she ran over to the tenor as he came toward her. She offered her small calling card for his signature, but he

dropped it in his pocket and autographed a program instead. He stooped and hugged her close, and then with an emotional face he left the room, refusing further autographs. The little girl has received several cards from him since. Could it be that she looks like another little girl somewhere in Russia, far from a lonesome blond father or brother?

My Russian friend was named Vladimir Schmakoff, and for several years I received postcards and Christmas cards from him. The last Christmas card he sent to me was mailed from nearby Fort Benning, Georgia, December 22, 1943, and his return address indicated that he was a Private in H.Q. Co. 176 Infantry. Mama tried to get in touch with him to invite him to come to see us when he had a pass. Alas, he shipped out without an opportunity to come to Auburn. After the war the Don Cossacks returned to Auburn in concert, but Vladimir Schmakoff was not with them. The conductor gave us an address where we could inquire into his whereabouts, and Mama learned that he had died. We will never know what attracted him to me, and I will always wonder.

Eight
A Sad
Life

OUR HOUSE ON DONAHUE DRIVE WAS MAINTAINED by Mrs. Cowart's son, Reuben*, who was responsible for the maintenance of all his mother's property. I remember Mr. Reuben as a gentle, soft-spoken person who seemed to have very little self-confidence, but there was an appealing wistfulness about him. He was a man of medium build with reddish brown hair and he usually wore a slightly misshapen brown felt hat. Although a bit eccentric and slovenly, he was always kind and polite. Sometimes his mother would be with him if he was just driving by or stopping briefly to assess needed maintenance. Mrs. Cowart was always courteous and pleasant, but I remember her as being more businesslike than warm and friendly. Like so many of the women of her generation, she wore her hair in a simple, easily managed style, and she usually wore a shirtwaist dress and sturdy, sensible shoes. In addition to Mr. Reuben, she had two daughters, Geneva Cowart Carpenter* and Flora Cowart Gaines*. As a child, I remember Mrs. Carpenter especially because Mama typed a thesis for her, and several times she drove out to our house to confer with Mama about her paper. She looked somewhat like her mother, not very tall and with chestnut brown hair, but I think she had a warmer, friendlier personality than her mother. My brother Norman dated Mrs. Carpenter's pretty and extremely popular daughter, Celeste*, while they were students at Lee County High School.

Mrs. Gaines's husband was a high-ranking officer in the Army, and they lived in faraway places. Their son, Harry*, used to visit his grandmother during his holidays from military school, and I remember him from the time we were in high school. He was one of the first boys in our age group to get his driver's license. Even more important, he was able to borrow his grandmother's car and take us all to ride. This was during the gas rationing of World War II so riding around was a luxury that few teenagers enjoyed.

GENEVA AND FLORA SEEMED TO BE ASHAMED of their brother Reuben and treated him as if he was not their equal. Their father, Dr. Bernard Cowart*, who died in 1935, had been very demanding of Reuben and was cruel to him in many ways. A close friend and neighbor of the Cowarts, Miss Dorothea Biggin, said that Dr. Cowart believed that the only way to make a man out of a boy was to make life hard for him, and he practiced this ruthlessly. Reuben was not allowed to have playmates, and he was required to come straight home from school and go to the pasture to look after the cows, even as a very small boy. Miss Biggin told of seeing him drive the cows home in the mornings to be milked, then drive them back to the pasture, and repeat the operation in the afternoon. She added that many times Dr. Cowart would drive along in his car, slowly, to watch Reuben carry a bale of hay on his back and shoulders from the house to the pasture to feed the cows. In addition to his back-breaking chores, Reuben was required to do excellent work in school. When he was about seventeen years old he had an illness or nervous breakdown, and Miss Biggin attributed this to the demands put on him by his father.

Many of the stories about Dr. Cowart indicate that he had a volatile disposition, and that his son bore the brunt of most of his outbursts of temper and outrage. Miss Biggin said that Reuben, no matter how hard he tried, could not please his father. She added that Reuben's friends loved him for his gentle, kind spirit, but these were the very traits that caused the most friction between the father and the son. Dr. Cowart was a brilliant scientist who was passionate in his devotion to his profession, but he resented any distractions from his work and research and he cared nothing for a social life.

Mr. Reuben Cowart drove a little coupe, and sometimes had a black man to help him. We always addressed him as Mr. Reuben or Mr. Cowart, and we treated him with courtesy and respect, because that is the way Mama had taught us to treat everyone, especially our elders. I wish we had known how much he would mean to our family in later years because I think we could have brought some happiness into a very sad life. Maybe we did without realizing it. I hope so.

Mama was at work on weekdays and also on Saturday mornings, so she was rarely at home when Mr. Reuben was there. He asked Mama, only once, to go to a movie in Opelika with him, and she declined saying that she never left her children. He said that they could take the two little girls, meaning Lamar and me. Mama still declined, but I'm sure she was polite and would not have hurt his feelings for anything. After our father died Mama had resolved to devote her life to her children. She was invited out by other men too, and corresponded with one or two, but she never had a date during her long widowhood.

MAMA DID NOT OWN A CAR UNTIL AFTER SHE RETIRED, so we walked to school and Mama walked to work. That was before we knew how important it was to exercise, but it didn't matter because we had no choice. If we wanted or needed to get somewhere there was only one way to do it. I've thought a lot of times that Mama's excellent health was probably due in part to her brisk walks every day, but her positive attitude and strong genes surely had a lot to do with it, too. We did have wonderful friends and neighbors who would watch for us and give us welcome lifts. The Jesse Neals could almost always be counted on to come by the house to give us a ride on rainy days.

Gay dropped out of college and married in 1940, which was a great disappointment to Mama. She so wanted each of us to graduate. Howard went into the Army Signal Corps shortly before Pearl Harbor, and Norman went into the Army Air Corps soon after that. So in 1943 there were only three of us children left at home, and Mama's life was somewhat easier than it had been. However, those were troubled times for everyone, and she continued to struggle to make ends meet. We were still living in the Cowart house, and it was that summer that Mr. Reuben Cowart wrote his will. He lived another twenty years, and I hope it gave him a lot of pleasure to know that he had done a wonderful thing for our family.

WHEN HOWARD LEFT FOR THE ARMY HE LOOKED everywhere to tell Bessie goodbye. Finally one of us heard loud sobbing from underneath the back porch. We found Bessie drowning her sorrows and wiping away her tears with her apron. Howard always loved to tease and Bessie was fair prey for his practical jokes, but she never got mad at him. The first time he came home on leave he was wearing his U.S. Army Signal Corps uniform and Bessie was proud and happy. She said, "Oh, don't he look pretty? He looks just like a porter on a train."

Nine
World War II

In January 1944 we moved from the Cowart house to 110 Miller Avenue (where the parking lot for the Auburn Alumni Center is now). It was just across the street from Comer Hall where Mama worked, and only three or four blocks from the high school. Wesley, Lamar, and I were the only ones left at home.

During the war years of 1941 to 1945 there was a great feeling of patriotism and pride in our country. The Red Cross asked everyone who could knit to volunteer to make afghan squares. My Girl Scout leader, Libba Duncan Pearson, had taught the girls in our troop to knit, and we made a number of squares. Some probably weren't quite square, but they still were used in making warm afghans for our brave soldiers. Miss Fannie McDonald, a favorite neighbor, had taught Wesley to knit, and he and I were able to teach Lamar. We proudly presented ourselves at the Red Cross office, but we left there disappointed because they refused to give us the necessary yarn unless our mother came with us. Mama did not know how to knit, but she convinced the lady in charge that we would make squares that would measure up to the most rigid expectations. We knitted up all the yarn allotted to us, and when we returned with our squares they must have passed inspection. From then on we could get all the yarn we needed on our own. The squares were all in olive green and were done in the basic garter stitch.

We advanced to the more demanding assignments of knitting socks, sleeveless sweaters, and gloves. These were more challenging and we turned out a number before we graduated to the even more complicated navy watch caps. They were made of dark navy wool, and they completely covered the head and neck, fitting down over the shoulders. There was a small slit for the eyes and nose. I don't remember how many of those we made, but I liked to think of our courageous sailors standing watch in caps that we knitted.

Many things, such as sugar, shoes, and gas, were rationed during the war. We weren't concerned about gas rationing since we didn't have a car anyway, and Mama said she couldn't afford any more shoes than we were allowed, but we did miss the sugar. We also missed our cow, which we gave up in our move from Donahue. Oleo came out to replace butter, and it was sold in white blocks that looked like shortening. Little packets of coloring came with each one, and we had to mix and mix to get that coloring worked in smoothly so that it looked like butter. Since we could tell that it wasn't butter anyway, we just quit trying to mix it up unless we had guests. The only company I can remember having was for Sunday dinner. There was a unit of ASTP (Army Specialized Training Program) students at the college, and members of our church were encouraged to invite the boys home after church each Sunday. I don't remember any of them in particular, but Mama did her part for the war effort by inviting two or three at a time as often as she could.

I was fourteen or fifteen when I got my first pair of stockings (there were no pantyhose back then), and these were held up with garters. The only hose that were available during the war were rayon, which meant that they were far from being sheer and they had a seam down the back which invariably got twisted and the stockings wrinkled around the ankles as the garters failed to hold them up properly. I can remember having on open-toe shoes once and looking down in horror at those hideous stockings working their way out of the toes of my shoes. Nevertheless, I felt terribly grownup when I went to the Auburn Methodist Church in my first pair of stockings.

NORMAN COMPLETED FLIGHT TRAINING and was commissioned a second lieutenant when he was only nineteen. Mama, Lamar, and I went to Columbus, Mississippi, for his graduation. We were excited over the train trip and also because it was the first time Lamar and I had stayed in a hotel. It is very likely that that was Mama's first time too. When Norman called the hotel to reserve a room, he told the desk clerk that his mother and two little sisters would need a place to stay. I was fifteen and Lamar was thirteen, so we were surprised to find a baby bed in the room. Norman said he must have referred to us as his teenage sister and his baby sister. Lamar was a good sport about it and even tried to sleep in the bed, but gave up on it after a few minutes.

Wesley graduated from high school a year early in the spring of 1944 and finished two quarters at A.P.I. before leaving for the Army on April 12, 1945. He was stationed at Fort Ord, California, and was thrilled that he would soon be shipped to the Pacific. No one ever wanted to go overseas more than Wesley did, and no one could have been more disappointed when an acute attack of asthma prevented him from going.

I GRADUATED FROM HIGH SCHOOL IN MAY 1946 with, as 'Fessor Parrish, our principal, always said, the best class he ever saw. There were four of us who had made all A's, so it was decided that Jim Beasley would be the Valedictorian and that Helen Edwards, Carolyn Hatcher, and I would be the Salutatorians.

Jim, the only boy with a perfect academic record, was also the only one who had started out with that class. The three of us girls, whose records were just as good as Jim's, had all skipped a grade. I doubt that it was a sexist decision because people back then didn't know the meaning of "political correctness." Anyway, I was glad to be one of the honorees, and it gave me an opportunity to spend some time with one of Auburn's most distinguished and beloved citizens, Dean George Petrie. He had served as head professor of history and modern languages, as dean of graduate studies, and he had started tennis at Auburn in 1888 and football in 1892. He arranged the first football game in the southeast —between Auburn and Georgia. After his retirement he wrote *The Auburn Creed.*

Dean Petrie helped me write my graduation speech on world peace, an ambitious subject but an appropriate theme as World War II had just ended. The speech, based on Isaiah 2:4 and Isaiah 11:6, was delivered with much fear and trembling but I made it all the way through. It was not very long, thank heavens, so I will include it here.

One World at Peace

The fundamental purposes of the United Nations, as set forth in the Charter, are to prevent future wars and create understanding among the peoples of the world. In order to make this possible, every individual must conform to the regulations of the United Nations Charter and thereby make this dream become a reality.

When a threat to peace arises, it should be removed or prevented before it becomes so large that it cannot be dealt with by peaceful methods. The United Nations has already been called upon to demonstrate this possibility. The disputes concerning Iran were settled by negotiating with Russia, who signed an agreement that all of her troops would be removed from that country. Only by the united efforts of all nations can powers deal with each other. For this the importance of collective measures is readily seen.

Recently there have been differences of opinion among the Big Four. These form the backbone of the organization, but, unless they remain united and on peaceful terms, the backbone will bend and break. We need not expect speedy agreement on major issues, but that member nations are eager to find peaceful settlements is an indication that we face a new era in world politics.

When controversy occurs, the Security Council will call upon the parties involved to seek a solution by negotiation, mediation, arbitration, or other peaceful means. Solved in this manner, problems are soon forgotten and possible wars may be prevented. These settlements must be made in conformity with the principles of justice and international law.

In one of his last speeches, President Roosevelt stated: "We are faced with the pre-eminent fact that if civilization is to survive, we must cultivate the science of human relationships—the ability of all peoples, of all kinds, to live and work together, in the same world, at peace."

It has been suggested that a world university be established where representatives of all countries could live together and understand the customs and beliefs of others. This would lay a solid foundation for the building of peace. Other schemes will be evolved.

Only as we understand that security comes from cooperative effort will we be able to build a world founded on the teachings of the Prince of Peace where the words of the prophet can be realized: "and they shall beat their swords into plowshares, and their spears into pruning hooks: nation shall not lift up sword against nation; neither shall they learn war any more."

Dean Petrie told me to practice my speech until I was sure I knew it, and then to practice it ten times more. Then he suggested that I stand in front of a mirror and repeat it out loud, and to do this at least three times a day until graduation. His advice has helped me get through many speeches and programs since then, and when I haven't heeded his advice I have regretted it. I had just turned seventeen, but I somehow knew that I was in the presence of a great man, and I have never forgotten him. He died the following year.

BECAUSE OF THE G.I. BILL AND THE TREMENDOUS number of veterans returning from military duty, the summer of 1946 marked the beginning of huge enrollment increases in colleges and universities all over the country, and Auburn was no exception. I had planned to wait until the fall to begin college, but Mama decided I had better enroll immediately before classes filled up. So I began on June 10, 1946—the day my sister Gay and her husband, Bob Smyer, had their oldest son and Mama's first grandson, Bill Smyer, at Drake Infirmary, A.P.I.'s Student Health Center. When Bill attended Auburn University, eighteen years later, he took a lot of kidding about being born in the College Infirmary. By 1964 it was strictly a student health service, and the labor and delivery rooms were a thing of the past.

My brothers returned from military service shortly after I enrolled in college. Fortunately they were entitled to the G.I. Bill, and that helped greatly with financing their education. Not only was their tuition covered, but also their textbooks and supplies, as well as a monthly stipend. By scheduling my math classes after Norman took the same courses, I was able to use his textbooks, slide rule, and other supplies, so I benefitted from the G.I. Bill too.

Those years in college were happy ones for me, and sometimes I regret finishing in just over three years. I went straight through, except for one summer when I served as a counselor at Camp Skyland near Asheville, North Carolina. I graduated with honors on August 27, 1949, when I was twenty years old. Because World War II interrupted my brothers' education, I was the first one of Mama's children to graduate. However, Wesley followed soon after, graduating in December of that year. It was a milestone for our family, and Mama was a very proud parent.

Good friends for fifty years: Nola D. Lane and Mattie Ellis, 1945

Lan Lipscomb in front of the A. F. Caley home in Marion Junction

Ten
Memories of
Good Friends

W HILE MABEL CALEY, OUR DEAR FRIEND and daughter of Mr.
and Mrs. A. F. Caley of Marion Junction, was teaching
first grade in Monroeville, Alabama, she met Wilbur Kelley, who
was the Assistant County Agent in Monroe County. He and
Mama had many associations through his work at the substation
and through Mama's as secretary to the Dean of Agriculture and
Director of the Experiment Station. She already regarded Wilbur
as one of her boys.

In 1941 she was delighted to learn that he and Mabel were to
be married. After serving in World War II, Wilbur was County
Agent in Dallas County (Selma), and then he was appointed
Assistant Superintendent of the Black Belt Substation in Marion
Junction. He was later promoted to Superintendent. Mama did
the payroll for all of the Alabama substations, and each month
she enclosed a personal letter to Wilbur with the Black Belt payroll. She was devastated when she learned in 1956 that Wilbur at
age forty-four had terminal cancer. She continued to write him,
but now more frequently and with words of encouragement. The
sufferings of this young family brought back memories of a

similar period in the life of our family, and she poured out her feelings in her letters. Mabel Caley Kelley saved those letters and many years later returned them to me, another poignant reminder of the close ties between the Caley and Ellis families. Mama wrote to Mabel and Wilbur on July 7, 1956:

My dear friends,

I've had you constantly on my mind for when I heard the doctors had found a tumor, and knowing that Wilbur had been having trouble for months, I just could not shake off my fear that it was found too late to do anything about it. Since I went through a similar experience, I realize how terrible it is to face the reality and to accept it. I only wish that there was some way I could be of even a small fraction of the comfort to you and yours that all the Caley family was to me during the hardest experience of my life, and their love and friendship has not faltered during the long, lonely, hard years since. I can truly say that anything that hurts the Caleys also hurts me very deeply.

I followed your courtship with much interest, as you know, and my love and respect for both of you has deepened through the years. Now, I rarely think of Mr. and Mrs. Caley but I think of "The Caleys," and that means their children and Wilbur, especially. I love, admire, and respect you, Wilbur, and with a deeper feeling than I have for many other good friends.

If my love and tears and prayers could help, your suffering would soon cease. If that can't be, I hope the knowledge of my deep feelings will bring a measure of comfort to all of you.

Love from your true friend,
Mattie N. Ellis

Mabel Caley Kelley Carlton in the Marion Junction Methodist Church. The furniture Daddy built ca. 1927 for the Sunday school was still in use in 1999.

MAMA ALWAYS SAID THAT THE GREAT DEPRESSION had little impact on our family because our income was so limited that we had nothing to lose. She remembered that there was one month while we were living in Pine Apple when our total income was $7. Everyone was struggling to make ends meet, and though members of the church could not contribute much to the offering, they willingly shared produce from their gardens and butter and eggs whenever they could.

Aunt Mabel sent fabric for Mama to make clothes for her children, and Mama remembers that she could not send her a thank-you note because there was not even a stamp in the house, or the penny or two necessary to buy one.

Although memories of Pine Apple were grim in many ways, Mama never forgot the friends who brightened her life and who added to the comforts and happiness of our large family. Lamar and I, the youngest of the six Ellis children, were born in the parsonage in Pine Apple. Dr. Erskine Donald deserves much of the credit for Mama surviving those two difficult births.

Mrs. William Fields was Mama's friend who encouraged her in many ways and discreetly provided material necessities whenever she sensed a need. After we moved from Pine Apple, Mama and Mrs. Fields corresponded until chronic poor health made it impossible for Mrs. Fields to write or communicate. While we were living on South Gay Street Mama received a large crate marked VERY FRAGILE with Mr. and Mrs. Fields's return address on it. Surprises, especially in the form of packages, were rare in our household, and we waited eagerly for Mama to get home from work that afternoon so we could see what wonders that box contained. It was a complete service for eight of Noritake china, and Mama was so overcome by such a generous gift that she sat down and cried—a rare occurrence for our stalwart little mother.

Bet Melton was a friend who could be counted on to lift Mama's spirits with her happy disposition and willingness to help with the overwhelming task of caring for all the little Ellis children. Frequently Bet would take Wesley and me to her house so that Mama could rest while her baby, Lamar, napped. On dreary, rainy days— always difficult times for households full of young children—Bet could be counted on to come sloshing through the rain and mud to bring cheer and welcome relief to Mama. Bet said that dark, rainy days were depressing for her, but the exuberance of our family dispelled any possibility of melancholia. Thus she gave the impression that she benefitted from those visits more than Mama did.

FOR MANY YEARS, MAMA'S CLOSEST FRIENDS in Auburn were Mr. and Mrs. J. C. Grimes, Mr. and Mrs. H. M. Lane, and Dr. and Mrs. H. T. Floyd. The Grimes family had been important to our family from the very first day we moved next door to them on South Gay Street in 1934. Their daughters, Betty and Mary Frances, have remained friends throughout the years, and I treasure many happy memories of times spent with them while we were children and later as adults.

Mr. Lane was farm foreman for A.P.I. He and Mrs. Lane lived in a wooded area on the campus, and we spent many happy Sunday afternoons visiting them and playing in the woods around their house. There was a hill nearby that was covered with pine straw, and we loved sliding down that slope in cardboard boxes. I guess that was as near to sledding as we ever got.

Mrs. Lane always had old-fashioned tea cakes for us to enjoy, and we hardly ever went home empty-handed. They were loving friends and were always generous with fruit, vegetables, eggs, milk and butter, or whatever they had on hand. I have enjoyed sharing many beefsteak begonia plants that were rooted from one very healthy plant that Mrs. Lane gave me years later. Many of the people who have these plants loved Mrs. Lane just as I did.

Soon after we moved to Auburn, Mr. C. J. Motley* told Mama that if she would buy her groceries at his store, he would give her a 10 percent discount because she was a minister's widow. She appreciated his offer and bought all of our groceries at his store on North College Street. Each month she received a bill for the total with a 10 percent discount deducted at the end. She never questioned his prices until one afternoon when Mrs. Lane mentioned that the price of sugar had gone up and named the new price. That didn't agree with the price that Mama was charged, so Mrs. Lane got out all of her grocery bills for the past few months. Mama went home and got hers, and they discovered that Mr. Motley had inflated the prices on Mama's bill before deducting the 10 percent, so she was actually paying full price or slightly more. It made Mama furious that she had been misled, and she didn't hesitate to tell Mr. Motley why she would no longer do business with him. From then on we bought all our groceries from Mr. John Turner Hudson, who could be relied on to deal honestly and fairly with all of his customers, including widows.

DR. AND MRS. H. T. FLOYD WERE STEADFAST and supportive friends during a particularly difficult period in Mama's life. In retrospect I realize that Mama was dealing with the fact that all three of her sons were in the military service during the 1940s, but it was also the time that she was going through "the change," as menopause was called then. Many times Mama visited with the Floyds on Sunday afternoons, sitting on their front porch and enjoying the support of these two dear people who treated her as a friend, but at the same time offered the kind of support that would help her deal with her anxieties about her sons. They suggested that swimming would be a therapeutic and relaxing exercise for Mama, and she took lessons at the A.P.I. pool, going two or three times a week during the evenings. She did seem to benefit from those exercises, and they were a welcome change from the stress of her normal workdays.

Mama had a lifelong fear of water, and those lessons helped her to overcome her fear. I asked her why she had that fear, and after a long thoughtful pause she answered, "Because you almost drowned when we lived in Centreville, and I still have nightmares about it. We had gone on a Sunday School picnic at a nearby river where there was a sandy bank and a swimming hole. There were a lot of people there, and I guess your Daddy and I each thought the other one had your hand as we climbed up the bank to leave. Gay dropped her bathing suit in the sand, and she ran back down to the river to rinse it out. She saw bubbles coming up and got a glimpse of a little hand. She grabbed you and pulled you out of the water as she screamed for us to come quickly. Your Daddy got there first and was able to get you to start breathing again, but Gay saved your life by finding you in time. I will always think an unseen hand had a part in it too. It was a terrifying experience that still causes me to have chills when I think of it. I'm glad you were too young to remember it." I'm glad too.

Eleven

Where There's
a Will

WE SAW LITTLE OF THE COWART FAMILY AFTER we moved from the house on Donahue Drive. I was invited by Dr. and Mrs. Frank Manley to a Christmas party when they were living in Cowart Castle, a lovely apartment building next door to the Cowart home. This was probably in 1952 or 1953. Reuben and his mother, Mrs. Cowart, were both at the party, and I remember pleasantly reminiscing with them about the years that our family had lived in their house. That was probably the last time I ever saw Mr. Reuben Cowart.

We learned later that in the early 1950s Mr. Reuben apparently started drinking heavily, but he stayed in his basement room and drank in seclusion. Perhaps he found in alcohol an escape from the miserable life that he had endured for so many years. One of his neighbors remembers that he was rarely seen during those years, but occasionally he would be seen hitch-hiking to Opelika, probably to replenish his supply of booze.

Mrs. Cowart died October 15, 1954, and I believe that Mr. Reuben's two sisters had him committed to Bryce, the state mental hospital in Tuscaloosa, soon after that. At a *non compos mentis* hearing they asserted that alcoholism had rendered their brother incompetent. At that time, Colonel C. P. Jones, U. S. Army (retired) and a very capable Certified Public Accountant, was appointed legal guardian to Mr. Cowart. This proved to be an excellent choice, and it was to Reuben's benefit that Col. Jones handled his affairs in a professional way, but also with compassion and affection for this man who had been shunned by some members of his family. He visited Reuben at the mental hospital from time to time, and those visits reinforced his opinion that Reuben was sane, and that he was a sensitive and caring person. Reuben appeared to be happier at Bryce Hospital than he had been in his own home, and he conveyed that message to his good friend and guardian, Col. Jones. Reuben lived the rest of his life at Bryce Hospital.

AFTER MY COLLEGE GRADUATION IN 1949 I could hardly wait to leave home and begin my life as a school teacher. I taught five years and had some rewarding, happy times teaching in Chattanooga, Tennessee; at All Saints' Episcopal School in Vicksburg, Mississippi; Bay Minette, Alabama; and in Suffern and Sloatsburg, New York. But suddenly I was overcome with homesickness and could hardly wait to come home to Auburn. Maybe I sensed that better things were in store for me, and that certainly turned out to be true. If I had not moved back I would never have dated and fallen in love with Lan Lipscomb. Although I had known Lan most of my life, I did not know him well. He was six grades ahead of me—almost like a different generation. When I moved home, I was twenty-five and he was one of Auburn's most eligible bachelors at thirty-one. My close friend from childhood days, Gene Hurt, suggested to Lan that he ask me for a date, and that was the beginning of our happy future together.

Mama was living alone in 1954 in an upstairs apartment at the home of Sgt. and Mrs. George Moxham at 120 South Gay

Street. Sgt. Moxham was called Sarge and he had a deep, magnificent bass voice that I will never forget. One song that he sang at the Auburn Methodist Church from time to time was *Rocked in the Cradle of the Deep,* and it was thrilling to hear him reach for those deep, deep notes at the end. He would sometimes ask me to accompany him on the piano, and we would have a little impromptu recital in the Moxham living room. Mama and Mrs. Moxham were an attentive audience and encouraged us to keep performing as long as possible.

Mama seemed happy for me to share her apartment, an arrangement that worked out well for both of us until Lan and I were married on June 3, 1955. Mama adored Lan and she was thrilled over our marriage. Lan always loved Mama and admired her greatly.

Lan and I first lived in a house nearby at 132 Burton Street which was owned by Lan's grandmother, Mrs. Isaac S. McAdory, affectionately called Mamadie by her grandchildren. Our three oldest children, Caroline, Lan, and James, were born while we lived in that house. In August 1960 Mamadie died at the age of 89, and we moved next door to her house at 301 East Magnolia Avenue. Several friends advised us to get professional movers and not try to do it ourselves. James was less than two months old, and when the movers were ready to move the baby bed, Lodie Wimberly, our beloved nurse for many years, picked up "her" sleeping baby and carried him next door, placing him gently back in his bed. She loved to tell him as he grew older how he slept through his first move.

After he graduated from college, our son Lan took a friend to meet Lodie and the friend asked Lodie how many children she had. Lodie replied, "Just four—Caroline, Lan, James, and Katherine." It was unusual for a black woman of Lodie's generation to be childless, but I don't think she felt deprived because she really did feel that our children were hers too.

This is Mama's story so I will leave mine and Lan's story for another time, but I felt it important to establish our situation at the time that a thrilling chapter in Mama's life began to unfold.

ON MONDAY, MAY 13, 1963, MAMA CALLED me after work and said that Flora Cowart Gaines had just called her and said she needed to talk to her and would pick her up at 5:30. Mama asked me if I had any idea what might be on Flora's mind, and of course I didn't have the slightest idea.

Flora picked up Mama, and as they drove to the Gaines home she said, "I guess you know that my brother Reuben has died." Mama replied, "Oh, Mrs. Gaines, I'm so sorry. I had no idea that he was sick or that he had died." Mrs. Gaines said that they had a private burial service and that it had not been announced in the paper. Then she went on to say that he was happy at Bryce and she spoke of what a burden he had been to her father and then to her mother after her father's death, adding, "Of course, you knew about that." Mama told her that she knew little or nothing about her family.

Then Flora said, "But I'm sure he must have embarrassed you many times." Mama said that he had never embarrassed her in any way, but that she had embarrassed herself once when she misunderstood his leaving a milk cow back around 1940. She went on to explain, "My cow had gotten out of the pasture, gorged herself on kudzu, and as a result died of bloat. Mr. Cowart learned of it when he was making repairs on one of the houses in the neighborhood. I think he felt some responsibility since Princess had broken through the fence, and he had always kept the fence in good repair. A few days later he brought a nice cow out and left her in the pasture that we used jointly with Mrs. Bessie Bailey and other neighbors. When I returned home from work that afternoon, I asked my children where the cow came from and they said that Mr. Reuben Cowart brought it. About that time,

Mr. Cowart drove up in the yard, and I very rudely told him that I didn't care to have him or anyone else try to manage my business and I didn't appreciate his bringing me a cow."

He was most embarrassed and explained that he bought and sold cows and had just bought a herd near Opelika and that this nice looking milk cow was in the herd. Since he raised only beef cattle, he had brought her out for Mama to try for a few days, and if she proved satisfactory, he would let her buy the cow for what he had paid for her. Mama felt terrible about her rudeness, and she apologized to him, saying that he could come back the following Saturday and she would pay him for the cow or he could take her away, depending on whether she proved satisfactory or not. The cow turned out to be better than the one that died, and Mama paid Mr. Cowart $60 and kept the cow.

By the time Mama had finished telling about the cow, they had nearly arrived at the Gaines home, and Mama asked Flora what she wanted to talk about. She replied that she was upset and would have to concentrate on her driving. As soon as they arrived, they went into a downstairs sitting room and Flora pushed a paper across a table, saying that she was shocked when she read it. It was a typed copy of her brother's will, dated July 1, 1943, in which he had left all of his personal property to Mama. His real estate had been left to his mother for her lifetime, but since she had predeceased him, this too was to go to Mama. *(See a copy of will in Appendix I.)*

Mama wrote in her account of these events, "I was completely stunned at the unexpectedness of such a legacy and at the insulting things that Mrs. Gaines said to me. She said, 'Of course, you can't possibly get any of it—no decent woman would accept money from a man on whom she had no legal claim—if you try to get any of it, people will say it was because you had sexual relations with him.'" At that point Mama let her know in no uncertain terms that she should be careful how she talked to her and what she said about her. No one had ever questioned Mama's morals, with good reason, and she wasn't about to let Mrs. Gaines intimidate her.

Miss Flora apparently could see that she had made a big mistake, and she tried to undo some of the damage by saying, "My sister and I know that you are a lady, Mrs. Ellis, and that you would not consider trying to get any of Reuben's estate, but we would be glad for you to have something—a thousand dollars—maybe two thousand—or even five thousand."

It was a one-page, concise will which had been drawn up by Joe Tyner, an Opelika attorney, and signed by Reuben Cowart on July 1, 1943. Mama tried to read the will as Mrs. Gaines kept talking, but she was so upset over the insulting things Flora had said that it was difficult for her to concentrate. She did ask where she got the copy of the will. Flora replied, "A lawyer was rummaging around in the Probate Office in Opelika and found it, and he brought it to me with the request that I engage him to contest it." Then she went on to say, "You know how these shyster, ambulance-chasing lawyers do—always trying to find something to pay them a big fat fee. Anyway, I would not consider employing him to handle anything for me." Mama asked her who the lawyer was, and she refused to say. She said that he was from out-of-town and that it was he (not she) who said that no decent woman would accept such a legacy and that no court would grant anything to Mrs. Ellis since they would assume that Reuben would have no reason to leave it to her unless she had had sexual relations with him. She said, "Judge Ledbetter* happened to be over here last night, and I talked with him about it. He also said that you would not have a chance of getting any of it because if you were a decent woman you would not accept it, and no court would grant it because they would assume the same thing the shyster lawyer did."

Mama told her, "You'd better tell your lawyer friends to be

careful about what they say about me." To that Flora replied, "They didn't mean you in particular, but any woman in general who might be left such a legacy. Geneva and I know that you are a lady, but your reputation would be ruined if the news got out that you had been named the beneficiary of the will, and that is the reason we would be willing to pay you a few thousand dollars to keep it quiet." She cautioned Mama to keep it quiet and said several times that they would rather for her to get a few thousand dollars than for some lawyer to get it, and that is what would happen if it went to court.

Thoroughly exasperated, Mama told her that she would make no commitment until she had had time to read and absorb the contents of the will, could talk it over with Carolyn and Lan, and perhaps consult a lawyer. Mama then asked her for a copy of the will. When Flora appeared reluctant, Mama told her that she would go to the courthouse the next day and copy it, or she could take it to her office that night, copy it, and return Flora's copy to her the next day. (There were no copy places back in those days.) Reluctantly, Flora let her have one of her three copies, and then Mama, anxious to leave, asked Mrs. Gaines to drop her off at our house. Mama was obviously shaken when she walked into our kitchen, and she told us to sit down before she showed us the will and then told us some of the things that Flora had said to her.

We were flooded with many emotions that night—surprise, disbelief, and excitement—but all of these feelings were clouded with fury that anyone would say the insulting things that Mrs. Gaines had said to Mama. Lan went with Mama to her office that night where she made several copies of the will, and then she mailed Flora's copy back to her the next morning.

In July 1943, when Mr. Cowart wrote his will, Gay had married and left home, and Howard and Norman were in the service. Mr. Cowart evidently had a lot of admiration for Mama, as

did most everyone who knew her, I'm sure. He realized that she
had worked very hard to keep her children together and to give
us opportunities at great sacrifice to herself. He also realized that
his sisters were well-provided for and they certainly would not
suffer if he left them out of his will.

In his will, Mr. Cowart had designated Emil Wright to serve
as executor. The signing of the will was witnessed by Mr. Wright,
Maiben Beard, and W. H. Sartin, all Bank of Auburn employees
at the time the will was signed in 1943. At the time of Mr.
Cowart's death in 1963, Mr. Wright was President of the Bank
of Auburn. While Mama, Lan, and I were discussing the will
and fuming over the insulting things Flora had said, Emil called
our house to see if Mama was there. He had called her house first
and since there was no answer he rightly assumed that she would
be with Lan and me. He made an appointment to see her the
next morning. I went with her, at her request, and he told us that
he wasn't sure that his other responsibilities would allow him to
serve as executor. He also felt that it would be necessary for him
to get approval from the bank's Board of Directors. He told us
that he didn't think there would be any problem because everyone connected with the bank appeared to be in sympathy with
Mama. We discussed some of the implications of the things that
had transpired, and then Emil arranged for us to see Knox
McMillan, attorney for the Bank of Auburn.

Knox was familiar with the contents of the will because Emil
had asked him to go to the Probate Office the day before and
read it. He said that he could not handle a case for Mama if Mr.
Cowart's sisters contested the will because he had been Geneva
Carpenter's lawyer for eight or more years. He had represented
her against Mrs. Gaines over some property after the death of
their mother. He said, however, that nothing would please him
more than to represent Mama if the case went to court because
Flora had tried to ruin him after he had represented her sister

against her and won the case. However, he stated further that he would not take a case for Mrs. Carpenter or anyone else against Mama or any member of our family because of his respect for Mama. He pointed out that if Emil agreed to serve as executor then he would be the one to engage a lawyer and that he would recommend Samuel Duncan* of Opelika, the county seat of Lee County, a choice that we heartily agreed with. We considered Sam a close personal friend as well as an outstanding lawyer, and our association with him during the next six months reinforced our opinion of him. Knox felt that it would be advisable for us to go ahead and call Sam, even though we didn't yet know whether the will would be contested.

When I called, Sam answered the phone and told us to come right away. That had never happened before or since; Lan and I usually had to wait at least a day or two to get an appointment. When we showed him the will, he was obviously pleased and very much interested. First of all, he told us to be discreet and not to discuss the matter with others. Second, he told us that Emil might choose not to serve as executor, and if that happened the court would appoint an executor. Third, the sisters might decide to contest the will, and in that event the executor would be the defendant because he would be defending the validity of the will, and Mama would be the beneficiary since she would receive the assets if the will was upheld.

A few minutes later, Emil called Sam and said he just didn't see how he could take on the responsibilities of executor. We were disappointed, but shortly after that he changed his mind and agreed that he would serve. Apparently the Board of Directors gave him clearance to serve, and we later understood that they encouraged him to do so.

When Emil called to tell Mama that he had decided to serve as executor, he had already talked to Sam and asked him to handle the case if it came to that. The next day I received a letter from Sam saying that he had been retained by Mr. Wright and that the will would be filed for probate in a few days.

Knox McMillan was a frequent visitor to Lipscomb's Drug Store as a customer and a good friend. His law office and our store were in the same block of downtown Auburn and across the street from the Bank of Auburn. Knox told Lan that Mrs. Carpenter had been to see him and tried to get him to handle the case for her, but he refused. Later in the day, Emil came to the store and told Lan that Mrs. Carpenter had asked him to give Mrs. Ellis a message. Emil said, "I'll give it to Lan Lipscomb, and I'll guarantee you that Lan will see that Mrs. Ellis gets it." The message was that Mrs. Carpenter and Mrs. Gaines were willing to increase the sum of what Mama considered "hush money" from five to fifteen thousand dollars. Then Emil said, "I told Geneva that I would give you the message, and now I have." After a pause, he added, "If I were you, Lan, I'd tell Mrs. Ellis to tell them to go to hell!" Emil also told Mrs. Carpenter that unless the court decided otherwise, and he didn't think it would, that she and Flora had none of Reuben's money to give. Mama had no idea of accepting their offer anyway. At that point she had no knowledge of the gross or net worth of the estate, and, anyway, after the way that Flora had talked to her, she was more determined than ever to make sure that her reputation remained beyond reproach. It is very likely that she would have seriously considered reaching a compromise with the two sisters had Flora not insulted her in such a demeaning way. Those indignities made Mama realize that she had no alternative but to do whatever was necessary to defend her reputation, and to do so in a court of law would not intimidate her in the least.

In a letter addressed to all of her children, Mama related the facts, beginning with her stormy session with Mrs. Gaines on Monday night. Then she wrote the following:

Thursday—May 16, 1963

This is not to ask for advice, and I don't want any of you to jump to conclusions and assume that I will inherit a considerable sum of money. I am going on with my work as usual and trying not to let it upset me unduly, but I must admit that it is not easy to do. If I should be lucky and come out with enough to provide me with a modest home and some of the better things of life that I have never had, I shall feel no hesitancy in accepting it. Knox McMillan stressed that there is no reason in the world why I should not have every penny of it—if I could get it—because a man is entitled to leave his estate to anyone or anything—the Red Cross, Salvation Army, various foundations, churches, colleges, orphanages, or deserving people. He said that it was a compliment to me and my children that we had treated Reuben with courtesy and respect when we rented from Mrs. Cowart to the extent that he would like to help me financially.

I want all of you to understand clearly that I am not counting on anything. I could accept the proffered "hush money" and be a little better off than I am at present, but everyone so far has advised me to hold out for a much better offer from the sisters or go to court. Emil and Knox both said that they know of no person in Auburn held in higher respect than I, but that Flora Gaines could embarrass me terribly and that she would not hesitate to do so.

Knox thought Mrs. Carpenter was going to contact me yesterday but she did not. If and when they approach me again with an offer to compromise, I mean to tell them that I will make no commitment until I know the full extent of the estate and on the advice of a competent lawyer.

Even though we had been very careful and had discussed this only with family and others who were directly involved, the word did get out. It spread quickly and it was certainly gratifying to learn that many people in Auburn were thrilled for Mama and furious with Flora.

On May 30, one of Lan's high school classmates, Gloria Hawkins Day, called Lan and arranged for him to meet her and her father, Chief Hawkins, at the Auburn Grille. Mr. Hawkins had been Auburn's Chief of Police for a number of years, including the year that the will was written. They told Lan that Mrs. Gaines had gone to see Chief Hawkins and asked him to round up witnesses who would swear that Reuben was an alcoholic and irresponsible. She told him that she would pay him.

Chief Hawkins was indignant and asked her if she was actually offering to pay him for obtaining witnesses for her. She immediately soft-pedaled her offer by saying that she meant to pay him for any expenses he might incur. At that point Chief Hawkins didn't know who the beneficiary was. Mrs. Gaines had told him that "some woman is trying to get everything Reuben had." Chief Hawkins said that it wouldn't do any good for her to have him subpoenaed because of his severe heart condition, for which he could get a physician's statement saying that he was physically unable to appear in court. Then Mrs. Gaines told Mr. Hawkins that she was sure he remembered taking Reuben home drunk many times, and he replied that he had taken a great many of the leading citizens of Auburn home drunk but that didn't mean that they were alcoholics. After Flora left, Gloria found out that Mama was the beneficiary, and she immediately called Lan and arranged for the above-mentioned meeting.

Twelve
There's a Way

THE WILL WAS FILED FOR PROBATE ON JUNE 11, 1963. Mr. Emil Wright and Maiben Beard (Mrs. Jeff) were asked to certify that those were their signatures on the will and that Mr. Cowart was normal when they witnessed his signature on July 1, 1943.

At the hearing for probating the will, Mr. Daniel Barker, Sr.*, as attorney for the Cowart family, entered the contest, signed only by Mrs. Carpenter. We were not surprised that they contested the will, but we were surprised that it was signed by Geneva only because Flora seemed to be running the show. There was a reason for it, though. Flora filed a petition at the same time to serve as administrator, and she could not sign both. However, her petition was set aside, and the First National Bank of Montgomery was appointed to serve as administrators until the case was settled.

The only people present at the hearing were the Honorable Ira Weissinger, Probate Judge; Samuel Duncan, our attorney; Mr. Daniel Barker, Sr. and Daniel Barker, Jr., their attorneys; and Emil Wright and Maiben Beard, who had witnessed the will and were employees of the Bank of Auburn at the time.

Sam Duncan told Mama that the following conversation took place during the hearing between Mr. Barker and Maiben Beard:

Mr. B.:	Were you standing or sitting when the will was signed?
Maiben:	Do you remember whether you were standing or sitting on a certain day twenty years ago?
Mr. B.:	Did Mr. Cowart appear to be of sound mind when he signed the will?
Maiben:	I had never met Mr. Cowart before that time, and I have never met you before now. Mr. Cowart appeared to be just as sane then as you do now.

We had heard that Mr. Barker, a greatly admired and respected lawyer in Lee County, was adept at throwing unexpected questions at witnesses, but Maiben did a wonderful job of answering them.

At that point we had no idea how much the estate was worth, but we learned later, shortly before the trial, that it included $70,000+ in government bonds, $25,000+ in stocks, and $28,000+ in mortgages against Mrs. Carpenter and Mrs. Gaines for real estate that they had bought from their brother. There was some accrued interest, making the total approximately $132,000.

Flora Cowart Gaines was a fairly tall, gaunt woman with unruly red hair, and she always appeared to be slightly dazed and flighty, but that was a misleading demeanor. She was well aware of what was going on all around her, and she was a shrewd, ambitious businesswoman. By contrast, her sister, Geneva Carpenter, was shorter, a little plump but pretty, and she had a pleasant face. Her chestnut brown hair curled softly around her face. Mama had typed Geneva's Master's thesis some years earlier and had found her to be courteous and easy to work with. Friends who knew both of the sisters were surprised that Geneva went along with Flora in the decision to contest the will, especially since they had fallen out over their mother's estate. This was the first time since then that they had joined forces.

Auburn was still a small town in 1963, and I felt that my family's relationship with the Cowarts, Gaines, and Carpenters was entirely friendly. In fact, Mrs. Gaines had had a bridal tea for me in the spring of 1955, and we learned later that she was aware of the will at that time. She and Lan's mother, Freddie, were not close friends, but they were in the same social circle, and Mamadie (Lan's grandmother, Mrs. Isaac McAdory) and Mrs. Cowart had been very close friends prior to Mrs. Cowart's death in 1954. We discovered that Flora had known the contents of Reuben's will when he was committed to Bryce Hospital soon after their mother's death. This came out in the trial during the testimony of Colonel C. P. Jones, who was appointed Mr. Cowart's legal guardian at the time of his commitment to Bryce. Col. Jones had the will in his possession along with other papers pertaining to Mr. Cowart's affairs.

LAN OWNED AND OPERATED LIPSCOMB'S DRUG STORE on College Street in Auburn, a business that his father had founded in 1922. Lan worked long hours, even opening for half a day on Sundays, and I was his bookkeeper. With our responsibilities at the drug store as well as at home we had little free time, but we discovered that we could and did find time for many additional responsibilities. That summer of 1963, following the filing of the will contest, was stressful, busy, and exciting for us.

Lan's sister and brother-in-law, Cora and Jim Swanner, were having an eventful year too. Their second daughter, Jeanne, was chosen Miss Graham, North Carolina, and then Miss North Carolina. It was a thrilling time for this family, and all of us, including Lan's parents, were in Greensboro for the Miss North Carolina pageant that summer. Her PaPa and Grandma Freddie wanted everyone to know that their beautiful granddaughter was Miss North Carolina, and they loved telling it to anyone who would listen.

Lan had a student employee at the drug store who commented to us, "You have the most exciting family I've ever been around! It's just like a soap opera, and I can hardly wait to get to work each day to find out what thrilling things have happened." But, at that point, 1963 was a long way from being over.

Cora and Jim's youngest daughter, Andrea, was badly burned in an accident in October. She was eight years old and was fascinated by a cigarette lighter that she had found. She must have known that she should not play with it because she hid in a closet to try it out. Before she was found and the fire extinguished she had suffered severe burns, mostly on the inside of her arm. So Cora and Jim were experiencing stressful times too while we were busily preparing for the trial which would begin the following month.

We hoped that the looming trial would not interfere with a trip to Atlantic City for the Miss America Pageant that fall. Mama offered to stay with our children, which helped make it possible for me to go. Lan felt that he couldn't be away from the drug store for more than two or three days, so he and his brother, Mac, made arrangements to fly while I drove our station wagon with my sister Gay to help with the driving. Our passengers were Grandma Freddie, Mrs. Homer Wright (a cousin of Lan's), and Mrs. Ben (Nell) Martin, a close friend of Freddie's from Clayton. We had a glorious trip with stops along the way for sightseeing. Gay kept a journal and promised to make a copy for each of the ladies. Mrs. Wright said that she could hardly wait to read it because she didn't have the slightest idea where we had been. Not surprisingly, we made frequent stops at comfort stations, as Grandma Freddie called them. Mrs. Martin always wanted to be the first in line, and then she would go again at the end of the line. She said that she always lived up to the motto, "Never pass up an opportunity." Those ladies were great fun to travel with, and we enjoyed lots of laughs and good stories.

Wesley called me at the hotel where we stayed in Atlantic City, and we must have made quite a splash there. When he asked the hotel operator to ring Mrs. A. D. Lipscomb's room, she asked, "Did you wish to speak to the grandmother or the aunt?" When we went to an elegant restaurant for dinner, the maitre d' asked how many were in our party, and I replied only the one word "five." He looked a little startled, I guess because I was able to get three syllables out of a four-letter word, and then he asked me what part of the South we were from.

Jeanne was selected Miss Congeniality, a title that she says goes to the candidate the other contestants feel is least likely to win. I don't think that is true, but I know we were all very proud of her, and it was a thrilling time for our family and friends.

When Jeanne had enrolled at Auburn University two years earlier she said that she knew only one other student and that was her sister Katherine. Then Katherine reminded her that when she had enrolled two years before that, she had not known a single person on the Auburn campus. Both of these favorite nieces found that they were soon involved in a variety of campus activities, and they gave their parents and grandparents, as well as their Uncle Lan and me, a lot of reason to be proud of them.

WE CONTINUED TO FEEL OPTIMISTIC ABOUT the outcome of the will contest, and the interest and sentiment on Mama's behalf were overwhelming. Many people offered to testify, and without exception, the ones that I talked to said in so many words that Mr. Reuben had lots more sense than his family gave him credit for and that he tended to his business as any man should have. Over and over we heard something like, "The only thing wrong with Reuben was the way he was treated by his family, and especially his father." No one seemed to hedge and each one volunteered information that I didn't ask for. By June 15, I had talked to Dr. M. W. Williams, Professor of Veterinary Medicine, and Cline Tamplin and Fred Hammock. Mama had talked to Mr. J. C. Grimes and Mr. H. M. Lane, our closest family friends. Dr. Williams told me that he used to test cattle for Mr. Reuben and that he was pretty sure that he could find records of those dates in the Bangs Disease Lab, which he directed. If those dates were anywhere near July 1943, that would be valuable information because it would indicate Mr. Cowart's diligence as a cattle farmer at the time his will was drawn up.

Later Mrs. Gaines went to see Dr. Williams and asked him if he remembered her brother. He replied that he had many contacts with Reuben when he inoculated his cattle and also tested them for disease. She told him that Reuben was completely irresponsible and had been such a disappointment to her father because he couldn't manage any of his affairs or take any responsibility. Dr. Williams replied that he knew Reuben as a cattle farmer and that he managed his farm better than most people. Mrs. Gaines then said that all she was doing was asking him to tell the truth, and Dr. Williams said that is exactly what he was doing—telling the truth. Naturally, Mrs. Gaines didn't ask him to testify for her.

Our good friend Margaret Arant told us that Flora had tried to enlist the help of Libba Duncan Pearson, whose father Dr. L. N. Duncan had been President of A.P.I. until his death in 1947. Flora and Libba had been lifelong friends, and their mothers were close friends. Libba refused to help Flora, and she urged her not to contest the will, saying that she was sure to lose and she would lose a great deal more in how people regarded her. Libba wrote Mama after the trial was over, confirming the fact that she had begged Flora not to continue her efforts to break the will. Mama had always felt very close to Libba and to the Duncan family, and she cherished her letter and sentiments.

Police Chief Fred Hammock told Lan and me that Mrs. Gaines had asked him to come to her house. According to Fred their conversation went like this:

> MRS. G.: You remember my brother, Reuben, and
> how crazy he always was, don't you?
>
> FRED: I remember him well, Mrs. Gaines. I used
> to see him often in the Auburn Grille after I
> returned from World War II. We drank coffee
> together on a number of occasions. But he
> always seemed sane to me, and he did a good
> job of looking after his farm and cattle.
>
> MRS. G.: I can see that you don't remember my
> brother at all, and your testimony will not
> be needed.

Fred asked us to have him subpoenaed because he really wanted to have the opportunity to testify as to Mr. Cowart's condition. He had enjoyed a close friendship with Reuben and would welcome a chance to testify that his friend was a sane, kind, generous man who had been mistreated and ridiculed by members of his family, especially his father. However, Fred was in military service during the early 1940s, and he did not return from overseas until 1946. His testimony would have been limited to a period at least three years later than 1943 when the will was signed, but he was helpful and happy to share his memories with us, and we certainly appreciated that.

Julian and Esther Berman owned Crest 5 & 10 Store, our children's favorite place of business. The Bermans both expressed surprise that Reuben Cowart's sisters had had him committed or that they would try to prove that their brother was of unsound mind in 1943. They added that he was a frequent customer of their store and that they had never seen any indication that he

107

was unable to make sound decisions. They offered to testify to that as well as to Mama's character and impeccable reputation. We expressed our gratitude for their willingness to help and for all the nice things they said about Mama.

The file on the *non compos mentis* hearing when Mr. Cowart was committed to Bryce Hospital in 1954 listed the reason for his unsoundness of mind at that time as the excessive use of alcohol. As far as we could determine, he did not start drinking excessively until the early 1950s.

Mr. Cline Tamplin, a close friend and former classmate of Reuben's, told us that they didn't have any business committing him when they did. He said that when Reuben got drunk, he stayed in his room in the basement, and he didn't bother anyone, and when he wasn't drinking he had more good common sense than his sisters. He also volunteered the information that Celeste Carpenter's husband, Tom Baird*, told him that he had taken Uncle Reuben from Bryce Hospital to Jackson, Mississippi, on business with him several times. Occasionally his business would take longer than anticipated, and if Reuben chose to return to Tuscaloosa, he would take a bus back on his own. Tom added that he never had a problem with Reuben and that he and Celeste and their children were all devoted to him. We had heard from several sources that the Bairds were thoughtful and attentive to their uncle's needs, and they frequently had him in their home in Birmingham for weekends and special occasions. Furthermore, he was capable of making these trips by bus and unattended.

Mama and I went to see Mrs. Bessie Bailey, who had lived next door to us on Donahue Drive. Her daughters, Frances and Frieda, were also there. We told them what had happened to date, and when Mama told them that the Cowart sisters had contested the will, Mrs. Bailey asked on what grounds. When Mama told her that we thought that they would try to prove that

Mr. Reuben Cowart was of unsound mind, she seemed shocked. She said that she had never had any reason to think that he was anything but sane, and she offered to testify to that effect. She was genuinely happy for Mama and sincere in offering to do anything that would help her. Red Meagher had come in the drug store the day he heard about the will. Red was usually the first to hear about everything. Lan always said that if Red hadn't heard it then it hadn't happened yet. Red said, "Lan, don't let anyone tell you that Reuben was crazy. I've known him all my life and the only thing wrong with him was the way he was treated by his family." Knox told Lan one time that Red was the best witness he ever had on the stand. He testified in a property dispute once, and when he finished Knox said there wasn't any need for the attorney to sum up the case. Red was the type to enjoy every minute of it too.

In a letter to my siblings the latter part of June 1963, I wrote, "I just wish I could tell you how people in Auburn have reacted to this, but I couldn't possibly quote everything that I have heard. I guess it boils down to this—people are happy for Mama that Mr. Cowart had enough respect for her and admiration for what she was doing to keep her children together, and he wanted to make it possible for her to have things that she could not have had otherwise, and people are angry with Flora for making Mama fight for it. Even people that I thought were close friends of Flora have expressed disgust."

Mrs. Aline DeBardeleben, owner of Polly-Tek (for many years Auburn's finest dress shop), rented the building next door to the Bank of Auburn for her store. The building belonged to Mrs. Cowart, and usually Mr. Reuben Cowart collected the rent. Mrs. DeBardeleben said that she would be happy to appear as a witness to testify to that fact and to say that he was always courteous and appeared to be perfectly sane to her. She added that she had never heard one word against Mama's reputation. A number of

109

years later I learned that Harry Gaines had gone to see Mrs. DeBardeleben's son Charlie to try to enlist his help. Charlie and Harry had played together as boys when Harry would come to Auburn from military school to visit his grandmother. Harry had asked for Charlie's help and advice, and Charlie told him quite frankly that he thought they should drop it. He added that there was no way the highly respected widow of a Methodist minister, who had raised six children all on her own, would not be believed by a jury. Charlie's advice went unheeded.

Professor Grimes, whose family was the first to welcome us to Auburn back in 1934, told Lan about a phone call, or rather two calls, that Flora had made to Mrs. Grimes. Flora started her conversation out by saying that people will stoop to anything to try to get something that did not belong to them. Mrs. Grimes interrupted her and said, "If you are referring to Mattie Ellis, one of the best friends I ever had, I want you to know that I don't appreciate the tales you have been spreading." About two hours later, Flora called and invited her and Professor Grimes to a dinner party—making no mention of the previous conversation and just as friendly as if nothing had happened. Mrs. Grimes refused the invitation.

I went to see Mrs. Doll Clay on October 10, 1963. She said that Mrs. Cowart and Reuben had eaten Sunday dinners at her boarding house during the war, and the only thing wrong with Reuben was that he had been intimidated by his family. Flora had already asked Doll to help her, and she had turned her down flat. Mrs. Clay had seen Reuben at Celeste's house just two or three years before he died, and she said he looked well and made a good impression. The most interesting statement she made concerned Miss Dorothea Biggin, a neighbor of the Cowarts, who was asked by Flora to testify that Reuben was crazy. Miss Biggin told her that she would not because she knew he was not insane and added that if he had been he could not have gotten into the Marines. I jumped at that and arranged for Mama and Sam Duncan and me to go see Miss Biggin that afternoon. As I was leaving, Mrs. Clay said that if there was any way she could help Mama she would be happy to do so. She had been very helpful, and I expressed Mama's appreciation and mine.

When I called Miss Biggin to see if Mama, Sam, and I could come over for a visit, she was very cordial and said she would be happy to see us. I told her the purpose of our visit and therefore no time was lost in preliminary remarks. Mama asked if it would be all right to take notes in shorthand, and Miss Dorothea said that would be fine with her. She added, with a little smile, "I don't think I have ever given dictation before."

Miss Biggin was frank and outspoken in her opinion of the Cowart family and the position of the two sisters in the present situation. She assured Mama that she hoped she would receive the legacy left to her by Reuben and added that her brother and sister felt the same way. Her brother, Lyle Biggin, had already gone to see Mrs. George Moxham, Mama's landlady, to tell her that he hoped "Mrs. Ellis would not budge an inch." He added that he had known Reuben all his life and that he knew he was sane.

The Biggin family told us much about the Cowart family. Miss Dorothea's observations, in particular, helped explain the remark made to us by many people that "the only thing wrong with Reuben was the way his family always treated him." She said that Dr. Cowart was a strong-willed man of short stature, and she felt that he made up for his smallness in body by being unusually harsh, especially with his family, and more especially with Reuben.

Miss Biggin was a tiny little lady who reminded me of a small fluttering bird. I was fascinated by the way she used her hands so expressively. She told us about the time when Flora (the youngest Cowart child) was a baby, and Mrs. Cowart had asked her husband several months in advance about visiting her family in

Colorado, and he agreed. She spent a lot of time getting clothes made for the three children, Geneva, Reuben, and Flora. Their bags were packed and the trunk was standing in the hall ready to be taken to the railway station. About an hour before departure time, Dr. Cowart came home and told Mrs. Cowart that she could go, but she could not take his children. She had to cancel her trip. Miss Biggin added that she and Mrs. Cowart were very close friends and that Mrs. Cowart confided in her many, many times. She was heartbroken over the cancelled trip.

Mrs. Cowart told Miss Dorothea that once when the children were small, Dr. Cowart was so harsh with the little girls that Mrs. Cowert had protested vehemently. He was not accustomed to having his authority questioned, but at last he agreed that she could raise the girls as she wished if she would not interfere with the way he handled Reuben. She reluctantly agreed to this, knowing that it was the only way she could protect the little girls, and if she had refused he would have continued his harsh treatment of all three of the children. Miss Biggin added, "When Reuben was a teenager, he did something that incited his father into a violent rage and he disciplined him so harshly that Reuben had what his family always referred to as a nervous breakdown. Right after that he spent some time at a mental hospital in St. Joseph, Missouri." It was obvious when she spoke of him that Miss Biggin remembered her friend Reuben with a great deal of affection and admiration, but with sadness too.

Not long before our visit with Miss Biggin, her sister, Mabelle Groves, who lived in Montgomery, had been in Auburn. When Flora saw her, she asked her to testify that Reuben was crazy. Mrs. Groves told her that she would not think of doing such a thing because it was not true. Then she added that she thought Reuben's money should go where he wished it to go.

Flora had already asked Dorothea to testify that Reuben was "always crazy," and she indignantly refused. In addition, she said that she had tried to convince Flora that she was hurting herself and Geneva by trying to prove something that was not true—that many people who had been friends of her family for years were disgusted with her—and that she had heard of a number of people who refused luncheon or dinner invitations from Flora for fear of being pressured into agreeing with her and supporting her in her claims.

Miss Biggin further told us that Reuben was never allowed to take part in any parties in their home and that his father made him wear bib overalls and eat in the kitchen with the servants, so he learned little of the social graces or good table manners. She said that he had been a sweet, lovable little boy who was devoted to his mother, but as he grew older he sometimes made it a point to do and say little things to irritate her. He had no patience with the Christian Science Church, of which Mrs. Cowart was a devoted member. He secretly began talking to a Catholic priest and seemed to get a great deal of satisfaction out of those visits. However, when Mrs. Cowart learned of them she was furious, and she gave the priest explicit orders never to speak to Reuben again. Miss Biggin, who was an Episcopalian, added that she thought Reuben could not agree with his mother on the Christian Science Church because he was too intelligent, and she also felt that if he had joined the Catholic Church, it might have given his life some purpose and meaning.

Miss Biggin told us that the first time she ever saw Reuben in a suit and tie was at his father's funeral in 1935. Even after Dr. Cowart's death, when Reuben received a portion of his inheritance, Mrs. Cowart and his sisters continued to dominate him, and they frustrated his every effort to be independent. However, Mrs. Cowart did start taking him many places with her, and for the first time in his life he had some social life.

We had already learned that Reuben served in the Marine Corps from 1922 to 1925. Miss Biggin asked us if we had heard about the reason that the Cowart family wanted to get him released. Mrs. Cowart had told Dorothea that their family thought it was beneath their dignity to have Reuben in the military service as a private when Flora was married to an officer. According to Miss Biggin, General Gaines seemed fond of Reuben and treated him better than his own family did.

Miss Biggin volunteered the information that the two Cowart sisters had a big hassle over their mother's estate. Knox McMillan had already alluded to this when he said that he had represented Geneva Carpenter in a dispute with Flora eight years earlier. Miss Dorothea continued by saying that Geneva felt that Flora was taking advantage of her and trying to get the better part of their mother's estate, and they continued to be very bitter toward each other until they joined forces to try to break Reuben's will.

Before we left, Miss Biggin said that Reuben must have admired Mama greatly and that when he wrote his will he was expressing his own wishes and intentions, knowing that for once he would not be repressed by his family. She wistfully described him as a person who lived a miserable life, but he was still thoughtful and kind in spite of a broken spirit.

She felt that he turned to alcohol because he had been frustrated and dominated in everything else he had ever attempted. She remembered that in 1953 he had spent several weeks at Hillcrest Psychiatric Hospital in Birmingham and that he did not take another drink for about a year. He was happy at Hillcrest because he was treated as a gentleman by the doctors and other staff members. The next time he went there, he and his sister Geneva had gone to a picture show at the Tiger Theatre while their mother attended a Christian Science meeting in the Bank of Auburn building. After the movie Reuben left Geneva to ride home with their mother, and he started driving to Birmingham. He had a wreck en route and was carried to Hillcrest Hospital. From there his family had him transferred to Bryce Hospital. He had a lot of freedom there and Miss Dorothea remembered that he was released a short time later.

After leaving Miss Biggin, Mama, Sam, and I agreed that she had given us valuable insight on the Cowart family and in the way that Reuben was treated by his father and his sisters, especially Flora. No one else would have had the close association with the Cowart family which Miss Dorothea had, and we appreciated greatly her willingness to share her observations with us. However, we felt that she would be a reluctant witness. It was obvious that she felt intimidated by Flora, and that fear would prevent her from saying many things in court that she had so willingly shared with us. We expressed our deep gratitude. I have kept that interview confidential since 1963. Now, almost thirty-six years later and twenty years after Miss Biggin's death, I feel that I can reveal what we learned that day.

MY HUSBAND'S PARENTS, GRANDPARENTS, AND great-grandparents are all buried in Pine Hill Cemetery, the oldest cemetery in Auburn. I remembered seeing the Biggin lot nearby and it took me only a few minutes to find it. When I looked down at Miss Dorothea Childs Biggin's grave to ascertain the year she died (1979), the inscription on her tombstone tugged at my heart: *Unto Thine Own Self Be True.* When she shared her memories of Reuben and other members of the Cowart family with Mama, Sam and me, I think she lived up to that motto.

MY BROTHER HOWARD, NOW A MASTER SERGEANT in the Marine Corps, was stationed in Hawaii during all of the time that we were preparing for the trial. He wrote frequent words of encouragement to Mama, and as always, his letters were interspersed with humor and good cheer. She saved these letters, and it was evident that they had been read many times. In one of them he wrote, "Don't let anything that Mrs. Gaines or Mrs. Carpenter say worry you. They might embarrass you temporarily but they cannot hurt you. I have heard that if anyone tries to pick a fight with you, you just tell them to go outside and start swinging and you will be there in a minute. Then you sit tight and let them keep on swinging all by themselves."

A few days later he wrote, "Just keep in training and stay fit in case you have to fight." Then he added, "Carol [his wife] is not trying to cut into your inheritance, but she did say that if you get a bundle she would like for you to get her another Danny Dozit. She got tears in her eyes when she pulled out the last one yesterday." (Mama's circle, the Wesleyan Service Guild of the Auburn Methodist Church, sold these little pot scrubbers to raise money for missions. They probably cost no more than 50 cents each.)

Thirteen
Discovery
Deposition

M AMA CONTINUED TO BE GRATEFUL AND AMAZED at the support and interest of close friends as well as people who
hardly knew her. In a letter to her children in early October 1963
she wrote the following:

> People who have volunteered to help since Carolyn's last
> letter include Ish [T. I. Jockisch], who quoted Mr. H. R.
> Hubbard as saying that Reuben Cowart had done the finest
> thing that anyone had ever done in Auburn, and that he
> hoped Mrs. Ellis would get every penny of Mr. Cowart's es-
> tate. That surprised me because I didn't know Mr. Hubbard
> even knew of me. Others include Julian and Esther Berman,
> owners of Crest 5 and 10; Dr. and Mrs. Glenn Schrader;
> Dean and Mrs. Roger Allen; Mrs. George Moxham; Dalene
> and Rennie Burton Jeter; Sarah Earl [Mrs. E. D.] Kirk*; Mr.
> Jack Cook; Mr. Jack Tamblyn; Dr. E. H. Walker; Mr. Thad
> Pratt; Mr. and Mrs. Rex Ditto; Mrs. Burma Stone; and Dr.
> Clarence Scarsbrook.
>
> The fact that part of Reuben's estate consists of mortgages

against his sisters is probably one reason they are so frantic—
they probably had no idea of paying them, but thought they
could put off payment until he died and then they would be
cancelled and they'd get the rest of the estate. Apparently
they had no idea he had willed anything to me. [At the time
Mama wrote this we did not know that Flora was aware of
the contents of the will and that Geneva probably knew
about it too. Flora had discussed it with Col. C. P. Jones at
the time of the *non compos mentis* hearing.]

Although the support is overwhelming, I can assure you
this has not been pleasant for me—I certainly won't say I
don't hope to get the money, and I can think of lots of ways I
could use it wisely and well, and would get a lot of pleasure
from it, but I have never wanted to be thrust into the lime-
light and I will truly be glad when it is over.

A letter that I wrote to my siblings October 17, 1963, began
by describing in detail our conversation with Miss Dorothea
Biggin and ended with the following account of the discovery
deposition:

The opposing attorneys took a discovery deposition from
Mama Wednesday afternoon. This type of deposition is set
up to determine what type of testimony and what kind of
witness will be presented by the opposition, and it is not an
unusual procedure. Sam Duncan will take similar depositions
from Flora and Geneva before we go to court. You would all
have been very proud of Mama on the witness stand. This
took place in the courtroom and those present were: Mrs.
Gaines, Mr. and Mrs. Carpenter, Mr. Daniel Barker, Sr.,
Daniel Barker, Jr., the court reporter, Sam, Mama, and me.

Dan Barker, Jr., asked all of the questions and he addressed Mama courteously and with respect. He started out

with routine questions as to her full name, age, address, when she moved to Auburn, Daddy's name and date of his death, where she has lived in Auburn and the dates, where she has worked and the type of work. He also asked the names of each of her children, to whom each one is married, where each one lives, and their occupations. Then he asked in what ways she had contacts with Mr. Reuben Cowart; if he came to our house for any reason other than to see about repairs; what kind of repairs he did. He also asked if she had many conversations with him; if she had ever done any work for Reuben such as typing; if he ever came to our home in the evening; if he ever had a meal with us; if he had ever discussed his finances, inheritance, or will with Mama. To each of these she answered "No."

To each question Mama gave an honest, straightforward answer—she did not seem at all nervous (although I'll admit that I was to begin with)—and it was obvious that her answers were spoken truthfully and that she had nothing to hide. She told about buying the cow from Mr. Cowart and the different types of repairs that he had made on the house. She was also asked if Reuben had ever appeared to be under the influence of alcohol or if he had ever asked her to do him a favor such as drive him around town, and of course her answers to both of these questions were "No."

Next Dan asked if Mama knew Mrs. Carpenter, if she had done any typing for her and when. Mama answered that she had typed Mrs. Carpenter's Master's thesis and she thought that was in the early 1940s. He asked then if she knew that Mrs. Carpenter's two daughters were living with her in Auburn. Mama answered, "Yes, my son Norman dated Celeste." We couldn't figure out why they would have brought up Mrs. Carpenter's daughters. That was the only reference to them.

119

The most exciting part came when Dan asked Mama how she had learned of the will, and she told of her meeting with Mrs. Gaines and quoted *all* of the things that Flora had said. I wish you could have seen the shocked look on Mrs. Gaines's face. She was trying to pretend that she had said none of those things, but I think she really was aghast that Mama would repeat them. Flora kept trying to tell Geneva that she had not said those things, but Geneva would not look at her and did not change her expression. Mr. Carpenter left the courtroom when Mama repeated the insulting things Flora had said to her, and he was obviously embarrassed. I have a feeling that her attorneys were finding out things that they did not know. Flora had told several people that she offered Mama $30,000, which was not true, and I think she must have told her lawyers the same thing because Dan repeated his questions about the offers she had made. I believe also that Flora had led her lawyers to believe that Mama had known about Reuben's will before his death. Dan asked several questions, each one phrased differently, about when Mama first learned of the will. He asked if she had ever discussed Mr. Cowart's affairs with Col. Charles P. Jones during the time that Col. Jones was Reuben's guardian; then he asked if she had discussed Reuben's will with Col. Jones before Reuben's death. Next he asked if she had discussed this "purported" will with Lan Lipscomb, Jr., or Lan Lipscomb, Sr. We can't imagine what was behind that except that Flora had told several people that her "good friend" Freddie Lipscomb [my husband's mother] was behind all this and that she wished her father was still alive so he could straighten Freddie out.

Lan's parents have been more discreet and have said as little about this as anyone I know. This is just another product of Flora's imagination, and I imagine that her lawyers

are getting fed up with the wild things that she apparently
has told them.

Mama even told them what Flora had said about a "shyster lawyer" bringing her a copy of the will and telling her
that no decent woman would try to get the money. She said
that Mrs. Gaines identified him only as an out-of-town
lawyer. However, we had no reason to think then, or at any
time later, that any lawyer had said the insulting things that
Mrs. Gaines related to Mama. Mama went on to say that
Mrs. Gaines had quoted Judge Ledbetter as saying that no
one would try to get the money because it would ruin their
reputation. Flora really squirmed when Judge Ledbetter's
name was mentioned. He probably would not have wanted
his name brought into this in the first place.

Sam told Mama when we left that he had never had a
better witness on the stand and that it was a privilege to
represent someone who can speak so truthfully because
there is absolutely nothing to hide. Sam had not thought
that Dan would ask Mama any questions about her meeting
with Flora but he was glad that it gave Mama the opportunity to get it on the record.

When we arrived at the courtroom for the discovery
deposition, Mrs. Carpenter came over and said, "Mrs.
Ellis, I just want you to know that I've always loved you
dearly. I would never say anything against you, and I
know you wouldn't be doing this if it weren't for those in-
laws of yours!" I guess Flora had told her that the
Lipscombs were behind this, and Mrs. Carpenter must
have believed her. However, there was absolutely no truth
to that, and Mama told her that she had been misin-
formed and that the Lipscombs were not behind it in the
least. Mama said that Geneva looked stricken as she
turned to go back to her seat. Perhaps she was beginning

to realize that her sister was the source of a great deal of misinformation.

We're pretty sure that the court case will take place the week of November 18 and that it will probably take several days. This will almost certainly be the star attraction of the fall term of court. We continue to be more encouraged every day, and there is no doubt in my mind that Mama will win. I just hope that this will be the last time we have to go to court.

CEL

IT WAS A SOURCE OF GREAT CONCERN FOR ME that the Barkers might attack Mama's reputation, although Sam had assured me that they were too smart for that. Even though many, many people had offered to testify as character witnesses on Mama's behalf, it did not appear that it would be necessary to present that kind of testimony. The only thing we had to prove was that Reuben Cowart was of sound mind on July 1, 1943, when he signed his will. Therefore, we concentrated our research on the people who had business dealings or other contacts with him about that time.

Fourteen
The Trial

THE TRIAL BEGAN ON TUESDAY, NOVEMBER 19, 1963, before
Judge Albert Hooton. The jurors *(see Appendix II)* were all
white males, with one from Salem and the other eleven from
Opelika. They were selected from a venire of forty-five jurors
(see Appendix II). The list included eleven men from Auburn, all
of whom we knew. We would have been surprised if any of them
had been chosen.

Twenty witnesses stated their opinions that Reuben Cowart
was of unsound mind, and nineteen witnesses declared that they
believed he was of sound mind at the time his will was executed
on July 1, 1943. In addition several depositions were read.

A deposition from Dr. Thomas H. Patton, psychiatrist at Bryce
Hospital, said Reuben Cowart "was not mentally competent when
he was in the hospital"; that he would not write his sisters and
wouldn't open letters from them; that he thought he had been
discriminated against in the division of the property; that he felt
that he had been "rejected."

The Cowart family subpoenaed Robert H. Svenson, who had
lived at the Cowart home in the early 1940s while a student at
Auburn; at the time of the trial he was living in Ohio. He and
Reuben had both lived in the basement of the Cowart home,

and most of his testimony concerned some experiments that Reuben was doing in which he kept human urine specimens in the refrigerator. He also told about an ant farm that Reuben kept in the basement. According to Mr. Svenson, Reuben was intensely interested in the ants and he spent a lot of time studying them and their habits.

Cora Askew, the Cowart's longtime maid and cook, appeared to have been well-rehearsed. Every question was answered in one of three ways: (1) Mr. Reuben has always been this way, (2) the real trouble started after Dr. Cowart died, or (3) the only thing that kept him out of the institution was his mother's love. It was apparent that she was very nervous, and when she stepped down from the witness chair she appeared greatly relieved that that was over.

The Cowarts' friends, Dr. and Mrs. Walter Schreiber, had testified on their behalf, although Mrs. Schreiber apparently had begged Flora not to ask her to testify. She had been a close friend of Mrs. Cowart's and a member of the Christian Science Church. Her testimony was very brief. Dr. Schreiber's was more detailed as he related that he was returning from New Orleans by train and Reuben, who was returning from overseeing the rice harvest on the Cowart plantation in Louisiana, was on the same train. Dr. Schreiber described their conversation, intimating that some of the things Reuben said suggested mental instability.

Several members of the Cowart family were called to the witness stand, including Flora's son, Harold Gaines, Jr. Harry, as he was called, was a major in the Army and he arrived in full dress uniform. Unlike Cora Askew, who had seemed to be very nervous, Harold was self-assured and appeared to relish the opportunity to talk about his Uncle Reuben in a demeaning way. He emphasized his uncle's slovenly ways, and he made the statement that it had always been very difficult for them to get Reuben to the barber shop.

Elbert Richardson, a black man who had worked for the Cowarts and occasionally helped Reuben with the maintenance of their rental property, was called to the witness stand. He was eighty-six years old and required help getting seated in the witness chair. In addition he was hard of hearing and his speech was almost incoherent. When asked how long he worked for Mrs. Cowart, he replied, "All my life." Then he was asked if he helped Mr. Reuben work, and he replied, "Yessir. He was crazy all his life."

Dr. James Ward, psychiatrist at Hillcrest Hospital in Birmingham, had been called as an expert witness by the Cowarts. In his cross-examination, Sam phrased his questions so skillfully that we thought Dr. Ward helped our case perhaps as much as he helped the Cowarts.

LAN'S FATHER, WHOM WE CALLED PaPa, HAD emphysema, which caused him to have severe breathing problems as well as poor circulation. Consequently his brain was not getting adequate oxygen, and his thought processes were severely diminished. Three years after the will contest we had an opportunity to encounter Dr. Ward when PaPa was admitted to Hillcrest Hospital for evaluation.

During the six days that he was a patient there, Lan and I took turns being with him a part of each day. One day I was in his room when Dr. Ward made rounds, and I asked Dr. Ward if he remembered testifying at a will contest in Opelika three years earlier. He looked a little puzzled until I reminded him that Mr. Reuben Cowart's sisters were trying to break his will by proving that he was of unsound mind when he wrote it. That jogged his memory, and he seemed to remember it. I then told him that my mother was the beneficiary of the will and that our family felt that he was one of their most effective witnesses.

THE COWART SISTERS HAD TRIED TO GET Geneva's daughter Celeste to testify that her Uncle Reuben was of unsound mind.

Celeste was devoted to her uncle and was kind and attentive to him when he was at Bryce Hospital. She refused to testify and told her mother and aunt that if they insisted, they might regret it. They continued to pressure her, and she climbed out of a window of the second floor of the courthouse, went down a fire escape, and fled to the home of a good friend in Auburn.

Mrs. Gaines and Mrs. Carpenter were dressed in their finery and wore hats and gloves each day of the trial. Though they appeared overdressed compared to the other participants, it was not as unusual then as it would be now. Those were the days when ladies wore hats, gloves, and even furs—if they had them— to football games.

Each sister took the stand, bringing up incidents from their childhood in an attempt to prove that Reuben was always crazy. They were both surprised when Sam questioned them about their brother's graduation from A.P.I. Both of them said that they did not know their brother had graduated. Sam produced a certified copy of Reuben's diploma and a copy of his grades, including the four courses he took in his final semester: Advanced German, Organic Chemistry, Economic Entomology, and Calculus. He made above a 90 in Organic Chemistry and similar grades in the other courses. When asked what she thought about his college record, Mrs. Carpenter said she thought the college just let him attend classes so he would think he was going to college, and at graduation she thought "they just gave him a piece of paper to make him think he had graduated because their father was a dean."

Mrs. Carpenter testified that at one time she had taken Reuben home with her to southeast Alabama to give her mother a rest. Mr. Carpenter had a lumber and planer mill and they tried letting Reuben work at the mill stacking lumber. She said that he could not do it correctly, so they decided to send him back home. They took him to the depot, bought his ticket to Auburn, and put him on the train. However, he did not get to Auburn, and they were worried about what might have happened to him until a few days later when his mother got his civilian clothes in the mail. He had gotten off the train in Montgomery, gone to the Marine Recruiting Station, and joined the Marine Corps. He served a three-year enlistment and was honorably discharged as was evidenced by the certified copy of his discharge paper which Sam produced at the trial. When Mrs. Carpenter was questioned about his serving in the Marine Corps from 1922 to 1925, she said that "it was so nice of the Marines to keep him for a while to give their parents some relief."

One of the stories Flora told involved raking leaves when they were children. She said that Reuben got mad and threatened to kill her. When Sam questioned her about the incident, he asked her when it occurred, and she replied, "in May 1912." Then he asked her what kind of leaves they were raking in May, and she tried to back down once again.

Both of the Cowart sisters brought out in their testimony that Reuben had first been committed to a mental institution in St. Joseph, Missouri, in 1909 at the age of seventeen. (Miss Dorothea Biggin had alluded to this earlier when she told us that Reuben had a nervous breakdown when he was seventeen.) Mrs. Carpenter testified that Reuben had an embarrassing experience at school, that he did not want to return to school, and when his father insisted that he do so, Reuben ran away from home for ten days. She ventured her opinion that "Reuben's mind snapped at that time and that he continued to grow worse." Then she said that as a consequence he was taken to St. Joseph for treatment.

Both Mrs. Carpenter and Mrs. Gaines testified that they had never once visited their brother during the eight or more years that he was at Bryce Hospital in Tuscaloosa, even after he was diagnosed with the cancer which eventually led to his death at the age of seventy-one.

The first three defense witnesses presented were Dr. E. H. Walker, Dr. M. W. Williams, and Professor J. C. Grimes. These distinguished men were professionals in large animal care and they had worked closely with Reuben Cowart in treating and inoculating his cattle. Dr. Walker was Assistant State Veterinarian and was responsible for testing cattle for TB and Bangs disease. In his testimony he stated that it takes a lot of judgment to handle cows, and it was his opinion that Reuben Cowart showed good judgment in the care of his herd of cattle. After a brief consultation with Harry Gaines, Daniel Barker asked Dr. Walker if Reuben Cowart was a cow-puncher. Dr. Walker replied that he would never have referred to him in that manner, but, he added, it takes a good man to be a cow-puncher and to put the cows through the chute.

Professor J. C. Grimes, retired Head of the Animal Husbandry Department at A.P.I., had worked with Reuben in Prof. Grimes's capacity as a Dairy Scientist. He also knew him as a competent businessman who was respected by others in the cattle industry as well as by the employees at the First National Bank. Mr. Grimes served for many years on the Board of Directors of the bank, and following his retirement from A.P.I. he served as President and Chairman of the Board of the bank.

These three men, Dr. Walker, Dr. Williams, and Professor Grimes, were articulate and provided valuable testimony concerning Mr. Cowart's capable handling of the cattle on the Cowart farm. We felt that they got the defense testimony off to an excellent start.

Mr. Thad Pratt worked for Auburn Ice and Coal Company, which also sold building materials. He had been a close friend of Mr. Reuben and had dealt with him as a customer. He said that Mr. Cowart always knew what he needed and seemed to manage his and his mother's affairs well. He couldn't imagine why anyone would think Reuben couldn't make a sound decision.

Earlier Mrs. E. D. Kirk* (Sarah Earl) had called to tell me

that when she and Mr. Kirk bought their lot on Sanders Street in July 1943, Mr. Cowart showed them the lot, pointed out all of the stakes, discussed the drainage, and pointed out one possible minor problem but suggested a solution for that. It was just the kind of testimony we needed. In addition, Mrs. Kirk was a lovable, witty person who would make a great witness, and she did not disappoint us. She was a pleasingly plump lady, and she expressed some concern about the width of the witness chair. I assured her that she would easily fit into it, although I was a little apprehensive myself. It was a relief when she did in fact sit down in it, and then she gave me a wink and a smug little smile. She bought a huge pink-flowered hat for the occasion, and her bridge club canceled their meeting that week so they could all come watch Sarah Earl on the witness stand.

Sgt. and Mrs. Rex Ditto, Mrs. Bessie Bailey, and Mrs. Burma Stone had all rented houses from the Cowarts, and they shared the pasture with us. They had frequent contacts with Mr. Reuben when he supervised the maintenance of their homes, and each one of them was an effective witness, testifying that Mr. Cowart managed the property well and that he was always courteous in his dealings with them. During cross-examination Sgt. Ditto revealed that he rarely saw a helper with Mr. Cowart and that he thought that Reuben did most of the work himself. Burma was Mrs. Henry Young at the time her family rented from Mrs. Cowart. After Mr. Young's death she later married Donnie Stone. She remembered Mr. Cowart replacing window screens and building a screen door for their house. She said he always drove his own car. She added that although he seemed very bashful, he was always polite and agreeable.

Mr. Levi Knapp, the former postmaster, had grown up in the same neighborhood with Reuben, and they were classmates all through public school and in college. He said that Reuben was "smart as hell" and that there was never a time that he thought

Reuben was crazy. His mother had always thought Reuben was a fine, sweet boy and was very devoted to him.

Mr. Cline Tamplin, who owned Tamplin Hardware, had frequent dealings with Reuben and he, like Levi Knapp, had grown up in Auburn. He had volunteered to testify for us and told us that he had refused when Flora asked him to testify for her. One morning, shortly before the trial began, Cline called Lan and said, "I've just come back from the bank and I have a message to call Samuel Duncan. Before I return the call I want to make sure that he is on our side." Of course, Lan assured him that Sam was indeed on our side. Cline was a member of a prominent family and greatly admired in the community. He was a little nervous on the witness stand but that didn't keep him from being effective and convincing.

Our next witness was Dr. Glenn Schrader, Chemistry professor at A.P.I. and a former neighbor of the Cowarts. Dr. and Mrs. Schrader were also neighbors of ours during the late 1940s when we lived on West Magnolia Avenue. We lived in a house owned by Mr. Shell Toomer which stood where Anders Book Store is now. The Schraders lived next door in a house also owned by Mr. Toomer and where McDonald's stands today. Mrs. Schrader (Inez) was the friend who gave Mama remnants to use for making our clothes in 1934, and she continued to give us fabric for many years after.

Dr. Schrader had known Reuben well as a student and as a friend, and he testified to that fact. When asked about Reuben's appearance, he replied that he was always conservatively dressed, very much like other men in the community. However, his most effective testimony came when Dan Barker asked him if he considered it unusual for urine samples to be kept in a refrigerator, and Dr. Schrader replied, "Not at all. That is where they are supposed to be kept."

Mr. Jack Cook, a plumber and longtime Auburn resident, testified that he had done a lot of plumbing repairs on Cowart property and that he usually dealt with Mr. Reuben Cowart, who was knowledgeable about needed repairs and always pleasant to work with. He remembered one time when Mrs. Cowart accompanied her son, and she had trouble deciding what she needed. Reuben told his Mama that she was wasting Mr. Cook's time, and he proceeded to make the necessary purchases with no further delays.

Mr. G. H. Carlovitz, Professor of Electrical Engineering at Auburn University, was a classmate of Reuben's and he had sat next to him in a surveying class. He said that Reuben was a smart, capable, and attentive student. When Daniel Barker asked him if Reuben took part in class recitations, Mr. Carlovitz replied, "No, none of us did. It was a lecture class."

Lan had talked to Mr. Jack Tamblyn who operated a meat market for many years. When Lan asked him if he had ever purchased beef from Mr. Cowart, he replied, "No, but I knew him well as a customer, and I had many conversations with him." Then Lan asked him if he thought Mr. Cowart was capable of making sound decisions, and Mr. Tamblyn replied, "Reuben was as sane as I am, and I know I'm sane." Lan asked him if he would be willing to say that to a jury, and he replied that he never made statements that he would not repeat anywhere. As Lan was leaving, he thanked Mr. Tamblyn, who said, "It is never necessary to thank a person for telling the truth, and I'll do just that—tell the truth—if I'm called on." He was a convincing person who spoke with firmness. It was apparent that he made a good impression on the jury.

Mr. Cecil Ward, owner of Tiger Motor Company Ford Dealership, came in our drug store just a few days before the trial, and when Lan asked him if he remembered Reuben Cowart, Mr. Ward replied, "Boy, I've been wondering why you haven't called me. Of course I knew him and knew him well. I considered him a very good friend, and there wasn't anything wrong with him except for the way he was treated by his family." (How many times had we heard that?) Mr. Ward continued, "He used to come by my place of business nearly every morning and we discussed a lot of things." Mr. Ward turned out to be one of our most effective witnesses. During cross-examination when he made the above statement, Dan asked him what kind of things they talked about, and he replied, "things like Auburn football, politics, and taxes." Then Dan asked him what he said about them, and Mr. Ward said, "He thought like you and everybody else in this room—that taxes were too high."

Mr. J. B. Richards, a barber, was a retiring, mild-mannered man, but he was a surprisingly good witness. When asked if he ever cut Reuben's hair, he replied that in the 1940s he had cut the hair of just about every man in Auburn and that he had cut Reuben's hair plenty of times. Dan asked him if Reuben was slow about coming in to get his hair cut. Mr. Richards replied, "Well, sometimes he would let it get a little shaggy, but he wasn't near as bad about that as his father was." There was no more talk about haircuts.

Robert Sims was Vice-President of the First National Bank in Auburn and his testimony was especially valuable since he had many business dealings with Mr. Reuben. He testified that Mr. Cowart had personal checking and savings accounts in the bank, and he had waited on him many times when he transacted business for his mother as well as for himself. In addition to that Robert was a willing and impressive witness.

A deposition was read from James Baker Moore, of Petersburg, Tennessee, who had managed a farm for Mrs. Gaines during his last two years in college. He remembered Reuben well, and they worked closely together in their duties as farm managers. He felt that Mr. Reuben was a competent and responsible overseer of his mother's property.

The trial had started on Tuesday and the final three witnesses on Friday were Colonel C. P. Jones, who had served as Mr.

Reuben's guardian while he was at Bryce Hospital, Mama, and Judge Tyner.

HENRIETTA DAVIS COVERED THE ENTIRE TRIAL for the *Lee County Bulletin* and she did a masterful job of reporting all aspects without appearing biased in any way. A number of our friends were there with us during most of the trial. Our minister, Powers McLeod, spent as much time as he could spare away from his duties, and Jim Woodson, Rector of Holy Trinity Episcopal Church, joined us frequently. His wife, Abbie, usually sat by me, and we both spent much of the time knitting as we listened intently to the drama unfolding before us. Both Powers and Jim observed that it looked like a wedding where people were seated on the bride's side or the groom's side, but in this case it was the Ellis side or the Cowart side.

Others were there, too numerous to name, who came not only to give moral support, but also to witness one of the most exciting trials that had ever occurred in Lee County. I would have enjoyed it more if I hadn't been so emotionally involved.

ONE COUPLE WHO ATTENDED THE TRIAL recorded their perception of Mr. Reuben, his family, and what motivated him to designate Mama as his beneficiary. On Thursday evening, after the trial had been in session for three days, they called on Mama to offer their encouragement, their support, and their admiration for her in the way she was handling a difficult situation. They shared with her their written evaluation. It was apparent that they had spent considerable time composing and writing this paper, and Mama treasured it for the rest of her life. I remember reading it soon after the trial ended. After Mama's death, I discovered it with other cherished papers, and I was reminded again of the beautiful way that these dear friends showed their support and compassion. It seems to reflect the feelings of many people in regard to Mama as well as the Cowart family, and especially Mr. Reuben. I think it is appropriate to include it here.

Reuben Cowart

His father, Dr. Cowart, had a brilliant mind, was aggressive, full-tempered, and personally regarded himself as a red-blooded he-man.

His mother was a shrinking violet as Reuben came to be. She did not dare to lavish upon her son the motherly affection he needed, nor to interfere in the cruelties to which he was subjected. She found solace in the literature and prayers of her religion.

His sisters accepted their father's belief that Reuben was a boob, heaped scorn, ridicule, and embarrassment upon him. Reuben inherited his mother's gentle disposition and his father discovered it early—much to his disgust. Reuben was relegated to the basement during early childhood and was subjected to many other cruelties, including severe whippings. He was practically an outcast in his own home and spent many lonely hours in the solitude of his basement room. Inevitably, he developed peculiar patterns of behavior which resulted in a reputation for being different or eccentric, and of which he became fully conscious when he approached maturity.

His enlistment in the Marines was a flight from the scorn of his family. The length of time he remained in that organization indicates a considerable degree of adaptability even to the rigors of military discipline.

His record in school and college proves that he was not mentally retarded, not a moron, not a boob.

In the Ellis family he found an oasis of good cheer, much fun, friendliness, and respect. (They called him Mr.

Cowart and very few other people did.) He was grateful. He recognized the heroic struggle Mrs. Ellis was making to keep her family together and to properly rear her children. He knew his family did not need any financial assistance from him, and he saw that Mrs. Ellis did need assistance. His making her the beneficiary of his will was a deliberate effort of a sane man to serve a useful purpose and to express his gratitude.

His alcoholism, which finally resulted in mental deterioration, was a flight from an unkind world which regarded him as being strange or different.

I TOOK MOUNTAINS OF NOTES, AND SO DID Henrietta Davis. Another person who did not miss a minute of the trial was Dr. Carl Benson, English Professor at Auburn University. He was so fascinated by every aspect of the trial that he kept voluminous notes and told us that he planned to write a book about it. He had arranged for others to teach his classes all that week so that he wouldn't have to miss anything. He observed that it had everything to make a perfect plot—adding that "it even had a witch who looks like a superannuated madam." We didn't ask him to elaborate on that. A few years later we heard that Dr. Benson had a degenerative brain disease and was a patient at Opelika Nursing Home. He died after a long illness. He had not been able to write his book, and when I asked his wife about his notes she told me that she felt sure they had been in the files at the English Department and that they would have been discarded when Dr. Benson retired.

FRIDAY, NOVEMBER 22, WAS THE FOURTH day of the trial, a day that would long be remembered. We knew that some of the most significant testimony was yet to be heard because the last three witnesses were Col. C. P. Jones, Judge Joe Tyner, and

Mama. When we returned from lunch, court immediately re-convened with Col. Jones on the witness stand. He was a retired Army colonel, a Certified Public Accountant, and Reuben's legal guardian at the time he was committed to Bryce Hospital. Col. Jones had the will in his possession and had known for many years what Reuben's wishes were. He was an excellent witness, articulate and impressive. He also gave some insight into the time that Reuben spent at Bryce. There they had many conversations in which Reuben said that he didn't mind being at the hospital. He had a lot of freedom and was treated well. Col. Jones had suggested that Reuben might enjoy a television in his room and that he would get one for him if he so desired. Reuben declined, saying that most of his friends would not be able to have one, and he didn't want any special privileges.

In his testimony, Harold Gaines had implied that Colonel Jones had said that Reuben Cowart was not capable of making a sound decision. After Harold whispered something to Dan Barker, Dan asked Col. Jones if he had ever made the statement that Reuben Cowart could not make a sound decision. Col. Jones very forcefully replied, "Young man, it is beyond the realm of possibility or feasibility that I could ever have made such a statement." Col. Jones told of his meetings with Reuben at Bryce Hospital, and said that he had asked Reuben to whom he was leaving his property and why. I quote from Col. Jones's testimony in court, "Reuben told me that he had left his estate to Mrs. Mattie Ellis because he knew Mrs. Ellis had had a very hard time as a widow trying to raise six children, that she had done it with a great deal of dignity; that he would like to do something for her and that what he had was not essential to the support of his own family." He went on to say that Reuben had explained to him that his sisters did not need anything, that they had been very handsomely provided for, and that he greatly admired Mrs. Ellis. He felt that his assets could make a big

136

difference in the life of a deserving person, and he didn't know anyone who was more deserving than Mrs. Ellis. He added that Mrs. Ellis and her children had always addressed him as Mr. Cowart, and he appreciated that.

Mama was called to the witness stand next. She appeared to be completely unintimidated, just as she was at the discovery deposition. She testified that she had moved to Auburn as the widow of a Methodist minister with six young children. She worked for Triple A (Agricultural Adjustment Administration) for $3 a day in the beginning and then became secretary for the Agricultural Engineering Department at A.P.I. at $98 per month. She moved in 1937 to a four-room house owned by the Cowart family. She testified that Mr. Reuben Cowart made repairs to the house and that her children were fond of him, although the only visits he ever made were to make repairs. She added that sometimes Howard and Norman, her two oldest sons, would help him fix the roof or make other repairs that required additional hands.

She continued to answer each question in a straightforward manner, and it was obvious that she had nothing to hide. I was not as cool and collected as Mama appeared to be, but her composure helped me to overcome some of my apprehension. I was very proud of her.

Mama had been on the witness stand for about thirty minutes when Gene Lowe, Sheriff of Lee County, handed Judge Hooton a note. The judge looked a little chagrined at the interruption, but he glanced down at the note. Then with a startled but serious expression, he rapped his gavel and announced, "Ladies and Gentlemen, the President of the United States is dead." After a stunned silence Mr. Daniel Barker, Sr. arose and addressed Judge Hooton, "Your Honor, would it not be appropriate for everyone to stand for a moment of silent prayer?" So Judge Hooton told everyone to stand, to bow their heads, and then, after a pause, he said, "Amen. The trial will resume." It was an electric moment in the history of our country, and the memory of it still gives me a chill because it came during a significant event in the history of my family.

For the only time in her long life, Mama felt that her reputation had been questioned and that her testimony on that witness stand was necessary to prove that her morals and integrity were beyond reproach.

When Judge Hooton announced, "The trial will resume," I was surprised because I had mistakenly thought that a will contest was a hearing and that only criminal cases were trials.

I did not keep notes on Mama's testimony, but I think a great deal of it had been covered in the discovery deposition. As I recall, Mr. Barker, Sr. was careful not to ask her too many questions about how she heard about the will. I'm sure he did not want a repeat of Flora's insulting remarks to her, but I believe that some of it did come out.

Both Mr. Barker, Sr. and Dan Jr. addressed Mama with respect and courtesy, just as Sam had predicted that they would, and I appreciated that.

Joe Tyner was a circuit judge in 1963 so he would have been the one to hear the case had he not drawn up the will. He, of course, was called on to testify that Reuben Cowart was of sound mind on July 1, 1943, when he signed the will. He was an associate in the law firm of Mr. Nim Denson in 1943, and Mr. Denson had a rule for everyone who worked for or with him, that everything pertaining to cases must be dated and either signed or initialed—even scraps of paper with a few notes on them—and saved. His secretary found the file that Mr. Tyner had kept regarding Reuben's will, and everything was there: the penciled outline of what Reuben's wishes were, the first revision, and then a copy of the final will. In addition to drawing up the will, Judge Tyner said that Reuben Cowart would come frequently to his office with and without his mother on business matters. He further stated that Mr. Cowart assisted in assembling figures for making out tax returns for the Cowart estate and that he came to his office in connection with platting a subdivision that his family was developing. He added that he wrote numerous deeds at Reuben's request for lots sold in the subdivision. "Mr. Reuben Cowart talked very intelligently and was no different from hundreds of other businessmen I dealt with," testified Judge Tyner.

This was the first time that Judge Tyner had ever been a witness, and it appeared that all the lawyers in Lee County had arranged their schedules in order to be present for Judge Tyner's testimony. They were not disappointed as he was a very effective witness.

I HAD SEEN JUDGE TYNER ONCE BEFORE WHEN I was called for jury duty and he was the judge. The first case that came up involved a robbery at a local grocery store in Opelika. The jurors were asked to raise their hands if they knew Mr. E. (the owner of the store that was robbed); if they knew the defendant; if they had ever been robbed; if they were related to or knew the defendant's lawyer; if they were related to or knew the District Attorney; and other routine questions which were designed to eliminate anyone who might be biased in this case. Finally we all trooped out of the courtroom while the jury was struck. I've never understood why they call it striking a jury when all they do is weed out some and put the remaining twelve on a list. Anyway, we were summoned back into the courtroom and the bailiff read out twelve names and each person whose name was called was supposed to take his or her seat in the jury box. There was just one problem. Twelve names had been called, but only eleven people had seated themselves.

Judge Tyner looked down over his glasses and instructed the bailiff to read the list again, and each juror was instructed to raise a hand when his or her name was called. When the bailiff got to Rosie Bell Dowdell's name there was no hand in the air. Judge

Tyner barked out, "Is Rosie Bell Dowdell in the courtroom?" and a weak little voice in the rear answered, "Yessir." The judge told her to approach the bench, which she discovered meant that she should come forward and stand before him. She was trembling with fright when Judge Tyner asked her if she had heard her name called out, and she nodded yes. Then he asked her why she didn't come forward and she said she had to take her baby boy to the doctor. To his credit, Judge Tyner softened his voice and his demeanor when he said, "Rosie Bell, we spent a lot of time trying to determine who should or should not serve on this jury. Why didn't you tell us that you had a problem?" And Rosie Bell answered that she didn't hear any questions about sick babies.

A YOUNG ASSOCIATE OF SAM DUNCAN'S PARTICIPATED with Sam in making the final argument to the jury. Though his notes have been lost, he remembers the theme of his argument which went something like this:

> Reuben Cowart was a perfectly sane, very compassionate, good man, although considered somewhat eccentric and a social embarrassment by some members of his family. If this Will is broken, the family members who mistreated him will inherit his money. His Will could have been written by him with bitterness, because of the treatment he received by some members of his immediate family. Instead, it was written with compassion and sympathy for a great lady he admired from afar; a lady who struggled alone to raise a large family and to provide her children with the best that she possibly could with limited financial resources. He could identify with her courage and her determination and left her his money simply as an act of kindness and admiration. His wishes and her good fortune should not be destroyed by an act of this jury in breaking this Will.

The jury went out about 5:30. We thought they would be out at least an hour or more, so it was a surprise when they came back after only thirty-five minutes. It was a tense moment as we waited for the verdict, and even when Mr. Floyd, the Foreman of the Jury, announced their decision, I wasn't sure that we had won until I looked at Sam Duncan's pleased expression. For the first time since the trial began I detected barely perceptible smiles among the jurors, and several of them looked directly at Mama with a glimmer of pleasure and encouragement in their eyes. Up to that time they had been very careful not to betray their feelings.

After all those months of anxiety the jury determined that the will of Mr. Reuben Cowart would be upheld, and we rejoiced for Mama that justice had prevailed. It was a victory for Mr. Cowart as well as for Mama and a time of celebration for our family and friends. We did restrain ourselves and tried not to show too much exuberance in front of the Cowart family. Mrs. Carpenter came over and congratulated Mama, and told her that she was happy for her. There was so much excitement and activity that I can hardly remember how anyone else reacted. I just know that we all felt a tremendous amount of relief, happiness for Mama and gratitude for Mr. Reuben Cowart.

The amount of the estate was approximately $132,000. Sam Duncan and his associates had taken the case on a contingency basis—if we lost they would get nothing, and if we won their fee would be 15 percent. Not only was their fee very reasonable, it was also reassuring that they had enough confidence in the outcome to take it on a contingency basis. Estate taxes took another 10 percent, leaving Mama about $100,000 plus accumulated interested.

SEVERAL MONTHS AFTER THE TRIAL, I WENT TO Davis-Dyar Electrical Supply Company in Opelika to buy a part that was unavailable in Auburn. It was a place that I rarely needed to visit, so I was surprised that one of the clerks looked so familiar to me, but I could not place him. Finally he said, "You don't recognize me, do you, Mrs. Lipscomb?" I confessed that I knew I had seen him and felt that I knew him well but could not place him. With a big grin he said, "I'm Dewey Yancey. I was on your mother's jury and I would have sat there 'til hell froze over!" He went on to say that he was sorry it took the jury so long, and I assured him that we were glad it wasn't longer. I told him that I kept hoping to get some indication of what the jurors were thinking, and they certainly did a good job of not betraying their feelings. He said that if I could have heard them in the jury room, all my anxieties would have melted away. He said that they would have been ready for a vote in ten minutes, but one of the jurors wanted to read a poem Reuben wrote that was presented by the sisters to show that it didn't make any sense at all. When the jurors started looking at it, they realized that the pages were out of sequence. After they were put in the proper order they discovered that the poem was really beautiful and well written.

Some years after the trial, Herbert G. Hard, Jr., identified himself as the juror who took the poem, arranged the pages in their proper order, and argued forcefully that Mr. Cowart was sane, even brilliant, and very compassionate. The poem was written on loose sheets of paper and only a few remnants could be found. In piecing it together it was obvious that much of it was missing. However, one verse emerged as an expression of Mr. Cowart's generous spirit and concern for those less fortunate. It seems appropriate to include it here.

> *We always have an idea that*
> *If we have more than we use,*
> *Then we are free to use it*
> *For the charitable benefit*
> *Of the unfortunate and worthy.*

Fifteen
Free From Worry

THE ESTATE WAS NOT ACTUALLY SETTLED UNTIL the summer of 1964, so Mama waited until then to retire. She was sixty-four years old, and it was a happy day when she could leave behind those long years of working. For the first time in her life she could look forward to some leisure time and not be burdened with financial worries.

She had always been frugal and handled her income sensibly, and she did not change her lifelong habits. She did, however, buy a small brick house for $18,500. It was on Sherwood Drive, a pretty street with wonderful neighbors, and she enjoyed her yard and garden as much as she did her home.

She had always loved gardening and was thrilled to finally have a place to exercise her green thumb. Her rose bushes gave her a lot of pleasure, and I was happy to have picking privileges. She especially liked the orange Tropicanas which bloomed profusely. She arranged them in a beautiful blue bowl, and she called that her Auburn arrangement because our school colors are orange and blue. She had many house plants that were given to her or that she rooted from clippings. One that gave her and all the

Mama with some of her retirement gifts in her Sherwood Drive, Auburn, home, 1964

Mama with Gay, Lamar, and Carolyn (front) and Norman, Howard, and Wesley (back), March 1969

Mama with Mark and Lamar Ellis Gilson and Lan Lipscomb, 1987

neighborhood great delight was a night-blooming cereus. It bloomed very rarely, but when it did it was a spectacular sight. Mama would watch the buds carefully and when they first began to open, she would call neighbors and flower enthusiasts to come see her plant in all its glory.

There was a beautiful, old-fashioned climbing rose on a fence nearby. The property belonged to Dr. Charles Isbell, and Mama asked him for permission to get some cuttings from the rose bush. He was delighted for her to have all she wanted, and she soon had great numbers of them rooted and ready to plant. She gave them to neighbors, friends, her children, and anyone else who wanted them. When I think of all the plants that Mama spread around I think of bread cast upon the waters.

One of her favorite plants was an Amazon lily, which has

large, glossy, dark green leaves and exquisite white blooms that smell divine. Mama later moved to Wesley Terrace, a Methodist retirement home and sadly it looked like the Amazon lily had not survived the move. I brought it home and put it out in my backyard under a tree, not knowing what else to do with it. It turned out that in my total lack of horticultural knowledge, I had done exactly the right thing. That plant came to life, revived itself, and by the end of summer looked healthier than ever and was covered with blooms.

Betty and Troy Patterson lived across the street and Mama loved them and their four children like her own. Once, in her late seventies, when Mama decided to change the light bulb on her front porch, she fell and was pretty badly bruised. Troy scolded her and told her she must never climb up on anything again. He was always there to help. They shared their time, their delicious home-cooked meals, and their beautiful flowers with Mama many, many times. They also kept a watchful eye on her and her house, and if they noticed anything out of the ordinary they would call me. That gave me a sense of security about Mama's well-being, and many times I had reason to be grateful for their attentiveness.

One of Mama's first purchases was a car, a blue and white Chevy II. It gave her a great deal of pleasure and a sense of independence. She had not driven a car since Daddy died, thirty years before, so she took some driving lessons and was relieved when she passed the test the first time. The following letter was written to her children July 7, 1964:

Dear Children,

I do not have the legacy in my name as yet but Mr. Emil Wright told me Saturday it should not be much longer before the inheritance taxes are taken care of and then it could be turned over to me. I do not know exactly how much it will be or in what type of securities, but I do know there are

some government bonds and that there is one note against
Mrs. Gaines and a mortgage against her and one against Mrs.
Carpenter. Mrs. Carpenter sent me a check for the interest
on hers but I turned it over to Mr. Wright since he is still
serving as executor and will until final settlement is made.
Their mortgages are long-term and at low interest so the income from that source will not be a great deal.

Mr. Wright told me I could get some money if I needed
it, but I did not plan to draw any until the estate was settled.
One of my first purchases was a pretty light blue Chevy II,
with white top and blue upholstery. I can't believe that it is
mine and that it is paid for! Lan filled the tank with gas for
me to initiate it.

I was especially glad that I went on and got it because
Bill Smyer [Mama's oldest grandson] and a classmate from
Daphne came up Sunday morning for tests, counseling, and
registration for the fall quarter. We met them at the train in
my car and Bill remarked, "I see Carolyn and Lan bought
another Chevy II." I didn't say anything, and Carolyn asked
Bill if he would like to drive it. Of course he did, and as he
got in Carolyn told him that this is Mama's car. He was so
excited that he hopped out like he had touched something
red hot. He said, "Grandmother, I'm not going to drive
your brand new car." He did, though. He and his friend
and I went out to Andy's Restaurant on Opelika Road for
lunch. That afternoon I insisted that he take his friend for a
tour of the campus before they got involved in tests, etc. He
was thrilled and I am too.

I bought the car at Dyas Chevrolet from Robert Williams. Some of you may not know why it was so important
to me to buy a car from Robert. Of course, all of you know
that he married Betty Grimes. Professor Grimes did more
legwork than any person in Auburn other than Carolyn in

an effort to see that I got the legacy. He was one of our best witnesses and so was Dr. Williams, Robert's father.

A few people have already asked me about donations for several different things. I give all the same answer—I can't make any promises until I see what my income will be. I honestly feel that I have inherited a sacred trust and I hope to spend it wisely and well. I hope to enjoy good health and live long enough to enjoy some of it but I will do some good with it too. However, I do not intend to start giving away any capital or making donations to this and that and maybe wind up like Miss Mary Cox did when she inherited a great deal more than I will receive. She spent it like water and like there would be a never-ending source, and now she's old and practically penniless.

Miss Mary Cox, whom Mama referred to in her letter, never married and neither her parents nor her brother ever let her manage money. When she was left with a sizable estate she was generous beyond her means and spent large sums very foolishly. When she died, one of her lifelong friends was her executrix, and there was barely enough left to pay Miss Mary's final expenses.

NOT SURPRISINGLY, MAMA DROVE VERY CAUTIOUSLY, engaging the turn signal at least a block before she planned to turn. She was a very willing chauffeur for our children and a tremendous help to me. Katherine, our youngest child and the youngest of Mama's seventeen grandchildren, was born in 1967. Mama was enjoying retirement at that time, and she spent many happy hours with her grandchildren, taking them to ball games and pep rallies, to visit her good friends, and to pick blackberries and plums wherever they were available. In 1983, when Katherine was sixteen and Mama was eighty-three, their roles reversed and

Katherine became a very willing chauffeur for her "Dabbo," as she was affectionately called by all of my children and Wesley's, as well as many of their friends.

After Katherine told me that Dabbo drove all the way from Auburn to visit a friend at East Alabama Medical Center, a distance of five or six miles, in the center turn lane, I was relieved that Katherine could take over the driving. She told her Dabbo that she was in the turn lane, and Mama replied, "I'm going to turn left when I get to the hospital." And that was that. Thank heavens no other driver needed that lane badly enough to challenge her right to it.

DR. B. F. THOMAS, SR., WAS OUR FAMILY physician from the time we moved to Auburn in 1934. In 1983 Mama wrote about him,

> He is one of the best friends my family ever had. He has been my doctor, my counselor, and my friend. I would put him in the class with Dr. Erskine Donald, to whom we owed so much during the three years we lived in Pine Apple. Because I was a minister's widow, Dr. Thomas never charged me for services with one exception. Wesley fell off an acting bar in the Grimes's backyard and broke his arm. I was charged $5 for four X-rays. Dr. Thomas was on the golf course playing in a tournament when he was called to his office to set Wesley's arm—a fact I did not know until later.
>
> He never made us feel that we were taking advantage of his generosity. Fortunately we were healthy and didn't require a lot of medical attention.
>
> The first time I had my blood pressure checked after I inherited Mr. Cowart's estate, I told Dr. Thomas that I could never pay him for all he had done for my family, but that I wanted to start paying him. He said he absolutely would not

charge me. I insisted and told him that he would force me to
do one of two things—either I would not come to him unless I was very, very ill or else I would have to find another
doctor. He looked at me for a long moment before saying
that he would charge me.

He may have charged me a little for professional services,
but he continued to offer freely the friendship that meant so
much to me and my family. I go to see Dr. and Mrs. Thomas
occasionally and sometimes take him his favorite dessert, an
angel food cake. *(See Appendix III.)*

Dr. and Mrs. Thomas showed their support for Mama during
the trial with frequent expressions of encouragement and support. She valued their opinions and their friendship.

When Dr. Thomas had surgery in Birmingham there was an item
about it in the local paper. Norman was living in Albuquerque at
the time, but he subscribed to the paper and he wrote Dr. Thomas a letter. Mrs. Thomas called Mama and told her that any
mother who could raise a son who would write such a nice letter
should know about it. She said that Norman mentioned several
instances where Dr. Thomas had been of service to one or the
other of us. Mama told her that she didn't know about the letter
but that she was happy that Norman wrote it. She added that we
all appreciated Dr. Thomas and wished there was some way to
repay him. Mrs. Thomas reassured her when she said, "Sometimes an expression of appreciation means more than money."

MAMA'S INHERITANCE MADE IT POSSIBLE FOR HER to give to worth-
while causes, especially those involving children. If she read in
the newspaper of a family's desperate needs because of illness
and a lack of money, she could be counted on to send a check
along with a note of encouragement. She was selective in the

contributions that she made, always making sure that she was donating to an organization that was well managed and that lived up to its promises and expectations. She never responded to telephone solicitations, and I have an idea that she made sure the solicitors who called her knew not to call again.

If one of Mama's children or grandchildren had a pressing need, she could be counted on to help, but only after she had verified the need, and she usually required that a note be signed. She said that it wouldn't be fair to her other children if she gave to some and not to others. However, she made some exceptions to this rule when one of her children did something that benefitted all the others, or when she had a vital interest in a particular child's achievements. There were several examples of this regarding Wesley's talents and some exceptional results of his endeavors. Wesley wrote and published a wonderful biography of our grandfather Ellis, incorporating memoirs that Grandpa had written of his experiences as a prisoner of war during the Civil War and of a trip to the Holy Land in 1904 for a World Sunday School convention. It is one of the finest family history books and genealogical studies that I have ever seen, and people who are not related to our large family have expressed that same opinion. It received a rave review in the *Mobile Press Register.*

Gabriel Richard Ellis, His Ancestry, His Life, His Descendants was completed and ready for distribution at an Ellis Family Reunion in Ocean Springs, Mississippi, in 1982. Wes organized and made the arrangements for this reunion of more than one hundred people, all descendants of Gabriel R. Ellis or married to a descendant. The book was a tremendous hit at this gathering of cousins. Mama had told Wes to keep up with all of his expenses in producing the book, and she would reimburse him for any amount not covered by the sales. She kept her word and happily wrote her check, saying that he had produced a family treasure and heirloom that all future generations of the Ellis family will cherish.

MUSIC HAS BEEN SUCH AN IMPORTANT DIMENSION of our family's life that I asked Wesley to write his memories of the year he spent in Birmingham and how that experience influenced his love for music. His account is included in Chapter Four, but it is limited to his grammar school years. Music continues to be an integral part of his life and Mama was so proud of his accomplishments that it seems appropriate to enumerate some of them.

Wes began playing the organ for the Sunday evening services at the Auburn Methodist Church when he was only fourteen years old. There have been few times since then that he has not had the responsibility for church music programs, many times as organist/choir director. He served a number of churches during the more than thirty years that he lived in Mobile, Alabama.

He took a temporary job at Spring Hill Presbyterian Church until they could find a permanent organist and choirmaster. Apparently they did not want to give him up because it took them twenty-one years to find a replacement. In 1970 he composed a Christmas cantata, *The Nativity of Christ,* which is scored for five-part chorus of mixed voices, harp, flute, harpsichord, and organ. He dedicated it to the choir of Spring Hill Presbyterian Church, to Marian Lee, harpist, and to Virginia Riedeburg, flutist, both members of the church. It was one of his crowning achievements, and in 1974 it was published by Harp Publications of California. In the fall of 1981, his publisher notified him that the cantata would have its European premier in Merzig, West Germany, on December 28, 1981. (It had already been performed on television in South Africa.) That was exciting news and Wesley began trying to arrange to be present for the performance in Merzig. Mama was almost as excited as Wesley was and she offered to pay his expenses. But it was not to be and she was as disappointed as he was when he called to tell her that he would be unable to make the trip. Mama never got over that and she always felt that he had missed what could have been one of the high points of his life.

To compensate for this disappointment to Wesley, Mama paid his expenses to attend the International Music Festival in Stuttgart, Germany, in September 1985. The festival celebrated the tercentenary of the births of Bach, Handel, and Scarlatti; the four hundredth anniversary of the birth of Heinrich Schultz and the hundredth of Alban Berg. It was the pre-eminent year for music in Europe and the trip was a glorious experience for Wesley.

He has written a number of published works and participated in many productions in Mobile, serving at various times as conductor, arranger, vocal soloist, organist, and pianist. One of my favorites was the musical play that he wrote for children, *The Bremen Town Musicians,* adapted from the book by the Brothers Grimm. It was produced by the Pixie Players and received many favorable reviews. Lan and I took our children and Mama to see it, and we all thought it was great.

He sang the role of Fagin in *Oliver* and the role of Pooh Bah in *The Mikado.* He played the piano accompaniment for *The King and I.* All three of his children, Leslie, Peggy, and John, played in *Oliver* and in *The King and I.* In addition to his participation in the performances, Wesley designed and made some of the costumes. Lan and I took Mama and our children to each of these events, and we never failed to be amazed at Wesley's remarkable and diverse talents.

Another time we attended a performance of the Piano Ensemble in Mobile. This consisted of up to twelve pianists performing at six grand pianos—truly an impressive sight. In addition to arranging some of the music, directing several of the numbers, and playing piano parts in some of the others, Wesley designed and printed the program. He also designed and built the podium. It was a magnificent evening, and one that received acclaim from the audience as well as the reviewers.

MANY TIMES MUSICIANS ARE CONFRONTED WITH unexpected problems, and they learn very quickly to make the best of them. These can be minor catastrophes, humorous experiences, or adventures that combine many unexpected elements. Wesley's experience in Costa Rica was an adventure that could have been catastrophic, but he can tell that story better than I can.

This is Wesley's story:

In the fall of 1991, I made a long-anticipated trip to Costa Rica to visit friends whose farm adjoins and overlaps the Monteverde Cloud Rain Forest. A few weeks before I was to depart, my friends contacted me with a request to do a favor for a group of young Costa Ricans by playing an organ concert for them. Their objective was to foster good music and aid in the restoration of some of the historic organs in their country. I quickly replied that I was not a concert organist, but if they would like a program of preludes and postludes (carried over from my almost fifty years as a church organist) I would be glad to oblige. I apparently misunderstood the request and thought it was to be a small informal gathering of friends.

A couple of weeks before my flight I was contacted by Sergio Bolanos, a young architect and organ buff, who was coordinating the program. When he asked me to furnish a biographical sketch for the radio, television, and newspaper publicity, I realized, to my horror, that this was not to be a small informal gathering in a modest church, but a full-fledged concert in the huge Metropolitan Cathedral in San Jose, Costa Rica. I was panic-struck and began wracking my brain for a way out of my dilemma, finally admitting to myself that there was no honorable alternative but to go ahead with the concert.

The organ on which I was to play is a big, beautiful Pierre Schyven instrument, built in Brussels, Belgium, in 1890, then reassembled in the cathedral in San Jose in 1891. My concert, therefore, was to be a celebration of the centenary of the organ's installation. Even the Belgian Ambassador to Costa Rica would be at the concert, a fact which only added to my nervous state.

This organ is almost an exact duplicate of a Cavaille-Coll, the great French organ builder of the 19th century and the preferred instrument of the composer Cesar Franck. I had already planned to play Franck's Chorale in A Minor so was able to register it exactly as Franck had specified in his manuscript.

I arrived in San Jose on Wednesday before the concert, which was scheduled for Saturday evening, November 16, 1991. Sergio met me at the airport and we went directly to the cathedral, only to learn that the organ had not been played for over a year and that it had a multitude of serious problems. One division was completely unplayable and there were numerous non-playing notes in almost every rank of pipes. But the organ "repairman" was there working on it and he assured us that there would be no problem in getting it ready for the concert three days hence. The repairman was actually a priest from a nearby village, and organ maintenance was his hobby. He was a dead-ringer for Fidel Castro, right down to his army fatigues, a full beard, and the large Cuban cigar ever-present between his teeth. I told him that I really needed to practice and to set my registration. He assured us that the organ would be ready the next day. So back we went on Thursday, only to be greeted with the news that he had run into a few more problems, but come back Friday. We had no choice but to comply. So Sergio and I spent the time that I had set aside for practice in sight-seeing.

On Friday "Fidel" (as I had begun to refer to our organ repairer/priest) had the same bad news for us—more problems. But surely, he added apologetically, it would be in tip-top shape by Saturday morning. By this time I was becoming thoroughly unglued over what I might have to play on. Added to the problems of the non-functioning organ was the fact that repair work and practice could only be done during the times when there was no mass scheduled, a problem of considerable magnitude in a large metropolitan cathedral.

Finally, on Saturday morning, the organ was in fairly good playable condition, except that Fidel had not been able to tune the reed pipes. Most of Saturday morning was devoted to masses for the people, with Fidel dashing in to tune a few pipes during the brief pauses between the services. I was a nervous wreck.

The first time I was able to play on the organ when it was in reasonably good tune and working order was at the actual concert on Saturday evening. Fortunately, I was so concerned about the organ that I had no time to worry about my lack of practice or about my performance.

The program proceeded, but not without its problems. For the J. S. Bach chorale prelude *Wachet auf (Sleepers Wake)*, I had selected the beautiful 8' Trompette on the Grand-Orgue for the all-important solo in this work. During the first appearance of the melody, the Trompette suddenly stopped playing—not just one note, but the entire rank of pipes. Sergio was my registrant. He immediately recognized the problem and drew another solo stop for the rest of the piece. I don't think anyone in the audience was aware of the potential disaster that Sergio averted, but by then I was a basket-case and played the rest of the concert on adrenaline rush. *(A copy of the program may be found in Appendix V.)* The attendance was estimated to be over 750 and apparently they were pleased since they called for an encore. I played the Bach *Toccata* and *Fugue in D Minor,* which had originally been scheduled but had been inadvertently left off the program.

Even with all the problems, it turned out to be a wonderful experience for me. Sadly, however, five or six years later Sergio and his parents were killed in a tragic automobile accident. I'll always treasure his friendship, the quiet but professional manner in which he organized the program, plus his invaluable assistance as my registrant during the concert. I could not have pulled it off without him. And I remember with much affection and pleasure the time I was a guest in the Bolanos home in Grecia, Costa Rica, a suburb of San Jose.

Mama never tired of hearing Wesley perform and she marveled that he could achieve so much while holding a full-time position at International Paper Company in addition to his many responsibilities as a church musician. He is a multi-talented person who is seldom idle.

WHEN MAMA RETIRED IN THE SUMMER OF 1964, Howard was in the Marine Corps stationed in Hawaii, and Norman was in the Air Force stationed in California, so Mama went to see both of them. She would not have been able to afford such a trip without her inheritance from Mr. Cowart. She kept a journal that is too detailed to include here, but I will highlight some of the things that I feel convey Mama's personality and interests.

Lan and I drove her, with our three children, Caroline, Lan, and James (Katherine was not born then), to Atlanta. We spent the night at the Marriott and had dinner at the Ship Ahoy, Lan's and my favorite Greek Restaurant. Sadly it is no longer there. As we were leaving the restaurant, I asked Mama if she enjoyed her dinner. I was surprised when she answered, "No, it was too expensive." When I reminded her that Lan had paid for it, she said that didn't make any difference because it bothered her for anyone to pay so much for a meal.

Mama wrote of her flight from Los Angeles to Honolulu, "I had a window seat and we flew into the sunset for about two and one half hours. It was the most beautiful sunset I have ever seen, and the lights of Honolulu made a welcome sight. I was met by Howard, Carol, and their five-year-old son, Marvin, and each of them draped a lei about my neck. My visit to Hawaii was a continuation of fresh flowers, festivities, and beautiful sights to behold."

She somewhat apologetically reported that she took a nap for several hours the first day she was there, adding that it was almost unheard of for her to take a nap in the daytime. She was relieved to learn that most people are affected by the abrupt change of climate and have what is called "Polynesian Paralysis."

From Howard and Carol's back door one could see the gap in the mountain where the Japanese planes flew on December 7, 1941. Mama and Howard took a boat tour of Pearl Harbor, and then they spent some time in the USS *Arizona* Memorial. Mama wrote, "It gives a tug at one's heart to look down through an opening at the center of the memorial and realize that the bodies of more than 1,100 men are still entombed there." She described in great detail the many wonders that she saw, and the terrible and sad statistics that emerged from that historic sight and that dastardly deed in history.

In addition to sightseeing with Howard, Carol, and Marvin, Mama made angel food cakes for them as well as some of their friends. She made the most delicious angel food cakes, from scratch and using a rotary hand mixer. She was convinced that they were fluffier and lighter than the ones made with an electric mixer, and I think she was right. She was famous for her angel food pies as well. These had a regular crust baked slightly, then a meringue layer directly on top of the crust, and finally a whipped cream layer which could be decorated with choices of fruit. She always made angel food pies at Christmas, decorating them with red and green cherries and a sprinkling of chopped pecans. The recipe for her Old Fashioned Dark Fruit Cake requires mountains of ingredients and several days of preparation, I would be surprised if anyone is inspired to give it a try. However, it was a major part of Mama's Christmas preparations for years, and I think just reading the recipe will give an insight into her personality. *(See Appendix III.)*

Wearing beautiful leis for her departure, just as she had for her arrival, Mama was looking forward to seeing Norman and his family, but she wrote, "leaving Howard's was an unforgettable experience—one of 'sweet sorrow'—and I had a big lump in my throat for a long time after the coast of Hawaii was out of sight."

MAMA WAS MET IN LOS ANGELES BY NORMAN and Susan and their two little daughters, Suzy and Danielle. A highlight of her visit with them was a performance of *Ramona,* which was an Indian story set in an Indian village.

Mama was always fascinated by Indians—their customs, culture, history, and crafts. She was born in the Territory of Oklahoma, seven years before it became a state, and there were many Indians living in and around Thomas, where she spent her earliest years. The children of Chief Howling Crane went to school with the white children, and she felt a special kinship to these people.

On April 27 Norman and Mama went to the Los Angeles Dodgers and Atlanta Braves baseball game. Don Sutton, formerly of Clio, Alabama, pitched a 4-1 victory for the Dodgers, much to Norman's delight. Later Mama would become a big fan of the Atlanta Braves, and especially of Dale Murphy. She rarely missed a game on television, and if someone was insensitive enough to call her while one was in progress, she cut the conversation very short. But the first Major League game she ever saw in person was that one in Los Angeles, and she never forgot it.

age 71

MAMA WAS HEALTHY AND VIGOROUS, AND remained so for almost thirty years after her retirement. In 1971, she and her good friend Inez Schrader went to Europe for six weeks. Mrs. Schrader's daughter, Lois, and her family were in Hargesheim, West Germany, a small village near Bad Kreusnach. Mama's account of this trip is thirty-nine pages long, all single-spaced. Lois drove them to many places, and they made a camping trip that took them through Holland, Belgium, and then by ferry to Dover, England.

retired in 1964

As I read her journal again, I was struck by the number of times they climbed up and down steps—undaunted by 77 steps to the top of Bath Tower, 67 steps down to the baths and catacombs, over 140 steps to the top of a castle tower, 127 winding wedge-shaped steps to the top of another tower, 101 steps in the spiral stairway of an old windmill, and detailed descriptions of findings on second, third, fourth, and even fifth floors of castles—all reached by climbing steps. She noted that the stairway leading up to the tower of Notre Dame Cathedral has 396 steps and the one coming down 476 steps. Mama was seventy-one years old at the time, and I think Mrs. Schrader was about the same age. Nothing seemed to slow them down, and they made sure that they saw everything.

An avid reader and student of history, Mama always pointed

out notes of historical interest in her travel journals, such as her reference to the Anne Frank House and the small yellowed scrap of paper on which Mr. Frank recorded the growth of his children. She noted that the beautiful cathedral at Aachen is built over and around the small chapel where Charlemagne began his reign as Emperor of the West in 800 A.D.

Mama's interest in music is also evident in her writings. She noted seeing a 755-year-old cathedral with a pipe organ of 890 pipes. She and Mrs. Schrader attended a half-hour service in German, which they did not understand, but they thoroughly enjoyed the wonderful organ and choir. She noted that music is the universal language. It can be enjoyed and appreciated whether you speak the language or not.

Her patriotism and her sympathy for soldiers are apparent in her writings also. She wrote, "Near the French border we passed Dunkirk and had a glimpse of the memorial at the cemetery there. It really put a lump in my throat."

In Luxembourg they visited the American Cemetery and she wrote, "Most of the 5,076 men buried here died in the Battle of the Bulge. General George S. Patton, Jr.'s grave is marked by a simple cross, but it is set slightly apart on a small grassy plot between the chapel and the main part of the cemetery, a fitting place for so great a man to be buried at the head of his army. I wept unashamedly as I stood there for I always felt that he was the greatest general we had. …My grief for him was not so much for his death as for the humiliation and lack of appreciation he suffered from many who should have supported him. However, I believe that history has vindicated him."

As THEIR TRIP WAS DRAWING TO A CLOSE, MAMA said that she tried to express her gratitude to Mrs. Schrader for making this trip possible for her: "Inez assured me that she would not have made the trip if I had not gone with her. She said that if Glenn had lived they would never have come for he would no more have left his lawn and mowing than he would have gone to Heaven in a handcar." This was Mrs. Schrader's first plane trip ever.

MY OLDEST BROTHER, HOWARD, WAS A RETIRED Marine Master Sergeant when he moved back to Auburn in 1976. He had suffered with chronic back problems for years, and following extensive tests, he was scheduled for surgery at Fort Benning Army Hospital in nearby Columbus, Georgia. The only problem was that he would have to wait for a number of weeks before they could take him, and he was in excruciating pain. Howard rarely complained but Mama could tell that his suffering was almost unbearable. She always tackled problems head-on, and in this case she went straight to the top. She called her friend Bill Nichols, U. S. Congressman and Chairman of the Armed Services Committee. She explained the situation in detail and asked Bill if there was any way that Howard could get an earlier date for his surgery. He asked for Howard's telephone number and in less than thirty minutes the Chief of Neurosurgery at Bethesda Naval Hospital called Howard and told him he could see him the next day. He had arranged for Howard to get a military flight from Maxwell Air Force Base in Montgomery, Alabama that very afternoon. I drove him to Maxwell Field and was surprised to find that they were expecting Howard and an attendant was ready to escort him to the waiting plane.

His surgery went well. He had excellent care, and he discovered that a Congressional referral ensures V.I.P. attention and red carpet treatment. The surgeon called Mama personally and reported on Howard's condition. Periodic reports were sent from the hospital, and Bill Nichols followed up by going to see Howard at Bethesda and then he called Mama to report on his visit. All Mama had requested was an earlier date for the surgery, but she and Howard were both thrilled that Bill had gone much further than that in making arrangements that even Mama wouldn't have requested or expected. Bill was a generous, capable man who served his country well in World War II, returning from that conflict as a disabled veteran. He was greatly loved and admired as he continued to serve his constituents in Alabama until his death in 1988. Mama may have been one of his biggest fans and she made sure that he knew how much she appreciated and admired him.

Bill Nichols was one of the students in the School of Agriculture whom Mama often referred to as her boys. She encouraged these young men at critical times during their college years and especially when she sensed that they were discouraged over their grades or an empty pocket. She corresponded with many of them during World War II and continued to keep in touch after her retirement. She was always thrilled when any of them came back to see her. Two of her favorites had distinguished careers as legislators and Bill was one of them. The other one was Pete Turnham who served with distinction for forty years in the Alabama House of Representatives, longer than any other in Alabama's history. He expressed his love and admiration for Mama in many ways, and she always cherished their special friendship.

MATTIE NORMAN ELLIS, AGE 91, 1991

Sixteen

Celebrations
of a Long Life

IN 1980 MAMA WAS STILL GRIEVING OVER HOWARD'S sudden death from a heart attack the year before, and we decided a big celebration for her eightieth birthday, February 19, 1980, would help get her mind on other things. I had an afternoon tea for her early in the week, inviting her friends in Auburn. Many times February is one of our coldest and dreariest months, but during that week in 1980 the weather was glorious. The sun shone and the temperature stayed in a range where we did not need heat or air conditioning. It continued to be perfect through the weekend. Family and friends from near and far came for a luncheon hosted by my siblings and me. Some of our generous neighbors offered sleeping space and our house was headquarters for breakfast, lunch, and supper for two days. Our cousin Katherine Lefoldt flew over from Jackson, Mississippi, just for the day because her husband's health was so precarious that she was afraid to leave him for any longer than that. There were fifty-five people here for Saturday lunch, but I don't remember many of the other particulars. I just know that it was an exciting time for all of us, and Mama treasured the memories of it for the rest of her life.

Mama was generous but not extravagant, and it gave her a lot of pleasure to be able to share with others less fortunate. She continued to be a good steward of her money, and she was able to manage her affairs and keep up with her correspondence for a number of years. She kept meticulous records and compiled all of the necessary information for her income tax returns each year. She wrote wonderful, newsy letters and she kept many of the responses that she received from family and friends. No one is more aware of that than I am because I have gone through countless boxes of them. Many of them are noteworthy, some of them bring tears to my eyes, but more of them make me smile or even laugh out loud.

In 1985 Mama's children gave her the best gift possible. Each of her children and grandchildren made a quilt square, and other squares were made signifying important events and interests in her long life. Lamar assembled the quilt and a friend of hers in South Carolina did the quilting. We presented it to Mama for Christmas 1985. It was her most treasured possession, and she loved showing it to her friends. She explained the background of some of the squares and why they were included—squares depicting Howling Crane, her night-blooming cereus, Dale Murphy and the Atlanta Braves, Auburn University football. A poem begun by Grandfather Gabriel Richard Ellis on the night that my oldest sister Gay was born, and continued by Daddy as he recorded the births of Howard, Norman, Wesley, Carolyn, and Lamar is a part of the quilt. It is in segments with portions of it embroidered on appropriate squares. *(See poem in Appendix IV.)* We refer to the quilt as The Quilt, as if there is no other. It remains a cherished family heirloom for her descendants as it tells much of our history.

In 1986 Mama had a pinched nerve that rendered her immobile for a time. After a few days in the hospital I moved her temporarily to the intermediate care section of Wesley Terrace

Lamar, Wesley, Carolyn, Norman, and Gay with Mama on her eightieth birthday, February 19, 1980

Mama with Toxey Hall, Neegie Williamson Smith, Katherine Ellis Lefoldt, Edith Williamson Purviance, Norman Ellis, Carolyn Ellis Lipscomb, Wesley Ellis, Lamar Ellis Sargent, Frank Bell, Lola Ellis Williamson (Daddy's sister), Mabel Norman (Mama's sister), and Gay Ellis Smyer, February 19, 1980

167

Mama with Michael Allen Sargent, March 1951

Mama with her grandchildren and great-grandchildren, February 19, 1980: Jody Jones and Katherine Lipscomb holding Kate Smyer (row one); Michele Jones, Alleen Sargent, Chris Sargent, Shannon Jones holding Adam Smyer, Suzy Ellis, Danielle Ellis, Peggy Ellis, Leslie Ellis, and Caroline Lipscomb (row two); Lan Lipscomb, Marvin Ellis, James Lipscomb, John Ellis, Dick Smyer, and Bill Smyer (row three)

Methodist Retirement Center. She was improving daily and I asked her to let me know when she thought she could manage at home again, and if Dr. Hagan concurred, I would take the necessary steps to move her back. She seemed to be dragging her feet each time I mentioned that, and finally she said, "I've been thinking a lot, and I believe the best thing for me to do is take one of the apartments in the independent living area of Wesley Terrace. It is getting more difficult for me to look after the yard at home, and there are repairs that need to be tended to." I was relieved that she had made that decision herself, and it took only a few days for her to select an apartment and to decide what furniture she wanted to move from her home.

She had lived very happily on Sherwood Drive for twenty-two years, but then she adjusted quickly to her new situation at Wesley Terrace. She already knew many of the residents there, and she quickly made new friends. She enjoyed having her meals with congenial people, but she enjoyed the privacy of her own apartment too. She and her good friend Ethel Wade were next-door neighbors. Ethel was also born in 1900, and I enjoyed telling those two beautiful friends that 1900 must have been a very good year for baby girls, and they were the best ones of all.

Soon after my daughter Caroline and her husband, Mike, moved back to Auburn, Caroline decided that she wanted to have a party for Dabbo's ninety-second birthday at her house and with her siblings as co-hosts. Caroline had assembled many family pictures and displayed them as well as the quilt mentioned above. This time they invited only friends from the Auburn-Opelika area because out-of-town guests would require a lot more involvement by me. Lan's health had deteriorated considerably, and I had my hands full caring for him. It was a unique experience, and a welcome one, for me to realize that my children were capable of making all the plans and carrying them out without my help. The invitations had indicated no gifts, but we were delighted that Jack and Jo Simms did not take that literally, because they gave the most wonderful gift imaginable. They videotaped the entire party, showing friend after friend as they arrived or as they greeted Mama where she sat in Caroline and Mike's beautiful den—looking like the Queen Mother. It was a joyful occasion, made more special by the permanent reminder given to us by Jack and Jo. So many times I have wished for memories of Daddy, of his voice as he spoke, or sang, or preached, but there was no such technology in those days. What treasured memories we are privileged to have in our present world of more technology than I will ever be able to understand, but I can certainly appreciate it.

IN 1988 WESLEY FOUND A WONDERFUL way to express his appreciation to Mama when he asked her to name her favorite hymns, and she readily named them: *How Great Thou Art, The Ninety and Nine, His Eye Is on the Sparrow, When They Ring the Golden Bells, In the Garden, Amazing Grace, The Old Rugged Cross, Silent Night,* and *Cradle Song.* Then as a surprise for her eighty-eighth birthday Wes arranged them for four hands: first as piano duets, and then as organ/piano duos. He presented the book to her and then he and I played all nine of them for her and her friends who had assembled for her birthday party. They are beautiful arrangements and many times after that we would play them for her, oftentimes on the organ and piano at the Auburn United Methodist Church. Wes and I frequently played duets in the sitting room of Wesley Terrace. It gave Mama a great deal of pleasure to invite her friends to enjoy these recitals with her. She never tired of our performances, and she especially enjoyed hearing her friends praise her children. Every mother loves to hear that.

Shortly before her ninety-third birthday Mama had a series of small strokes and it was necessary to move her to the nursing wing of Wesley Terrace. Most of the time she sat quietly in her chair, dozing off and on and showing little interest in her sur-roundings, but she always knew her children and grandchildren. On May 31, 1993, she died peacefully in her sleep. She was ninety-three years old and had been a widow for sixty years and two months.

Wesley, Lamar, and I played some of Wesley's organ/piano duo arrangements at Mama's funeral. Wesley played the organ, and Lamar and I each had a turn at the piano. It was very emo-tional, and we weren't sure we could do it. Knowing that it would have pleased Mama so much helped us get through it.

Wes played for the entire service. He and Lamar played Mama's favorite, *How Great Thou Art*. He and I played *In the Garden* (my favorite) and *His Eye Is on the Sparrow* (Daddy's favorite). The service was in the Auburn United Methodist Church. Our minister, Dr. George Mathison, and our former minister, the Reverend Charles Britt, were greatly loved and admired by Mama. Each of them shared their own beautiful memories of Mama and they spoke words of encouragement to her children. It was a glorious celebration of a life well lived, and we were grateful for the many friends and relatives who were there to share their memories of Mama and to express their love and sympathy.

MAMA HAD LIVED IN AUBURN FOR ALMOST SIXTY years, and she had expressed her wish to be buried here rather than in Selma next to Daddy. They had never lived in Selma, although they had spent four long months there during Daddy's final illness. The generos-ity of Mr. and Mrs. T. J. Jackson in giving the lot for Daddy's grave was always greatly appreciated by Mama. We carried out her wishes and buried her in Auburn in the Memorial Park Cemetery. After-ward my siblings and I agreed that we wanted Daddy remembered along with her, and we placed a marker for him on the space next to Mama's.

The inscriptions read:

Mattie Norman Ellis
ADORED WIFE, MOTHER AND GRANDMOTHER
Feb. 19, 1900 - May 31, 1993

Rev. Henry Marvin Ellis
BURIED IN SELMA, ALABAMA
April 5, 1884 - March 31, 1933

AFTER MAMA'S DEATH I FOUND A NUMBER of letters that she received during those stressful months of 1963, but the one that she obviously had read most often was from Howard, my oldest brother and a Master Sergeant in the Marine Corps. He was stationed in Hawaii during the time that we were preparing for the trial and for those memorable four days that we were in court. He wrote Mama frequent letters of encouragement and support. We called him as soon as we got home from the trial to tell him the verdict, and of course he was jubilant. Within minutes of our call, he composed a letter to Mama. He was the one who was "not scholarly" and his schooling got off to a bad start, but he expressed his reaction better than anyone else, and at the same time paid a beautiful tribute to Mama and to Mr. Reuben Cowart as well.

Dear Mama,

The feeling that I experienced just thirty minutes ago must be mild in comparison to what you felt when the jury announced their decision. I knew you would win, but still I was in knots all week. It proves that the just will be rewarded.

Mama, when the jury brought out their verdict in favor of you, they also elevated Mr. Reuben to a respectful and honored position, a place his family had tried so hard to keep

him from getting, and a place he long deserved. I believe he
is as happy today as you are.

Love,
Howard
Nov. 22, 1963

After I wrote this story for my children, as well as my siblings
and nieces and nephews, I asked several of my friends to read the
first draft. These were people whose opinions I valued, and they
were also friends, or children of friends, of Mama's. One person
whose parents had been true and steadfast supporters for many
years wrote a beautiful and eloquent appraisal and generously
gave me permission to close my story with it:

> It is a story which has both a hero and a heroine. It beauti-
> fully portrays what a remarkable woman your mother was and
> reflects a steadfastness and character which few humans have.
> Her determination to keep her family together under such ad-
> verse circumstances, and her success in raising and educating a
> family of outstanding individuals, has resulted in a legacy of
> pride which you and your brothers and sisters will always have
> to remember her by. I know of no greater legacy which a par-
> ent can leave to his or her children.
>
> Mr. Cowart, the hero, was clearly a man of compassion in
> spite of the adversity under which he had lived all of his life. In
> a very quiet way and knowing that he would receive no thanks
> personally, he arranged a reward to a person he so clearly ad-
> mired and who was so deserving of the gift. I cannot imagine
> that for his sake the justice system could have arrived at a dif-
> ferent decision.
>
> One of the experiences in your mother's life which I
> found particularly moving was the reduction in her widow's
> pension engineered by the local minister because her children

appeared to be overdressed. Your mother's desire to present her children in the best fashion possible was another reflection of her pride and dignity and her willingness to spend many hours sewing and working in other ways to accomplish it. It also reflects that a so-called "man of God" had so little insight and was unable to see her qualities as Mr. Cowart, an alcoholic and misfit in so many people's eyes, saw her. It is her sense of pride and self-respect which makes her story so profound and should be at the heart of any way it is presented.

I hope you will find a way to publish this story. . . . I think our welfare oriented, dependent-on-somebody-else society needs to hear this story of a person succeeding under adversities which do not exist today, and depending on her own initiative, perseverance and faith to succeed without the help of government agencies. I think such a story would be well received.

Many years ago Mother told me of the legacy Mr. Cowart left to your mother and the ensuing litigation, but I knew nothing of the details and the difficulties your family went through.

Mother and Daddy both spoke on many occasions of the special friendship with your mother, and though I did not know her well personally, I remember her fondly. I am delighted to know her so much better through your account, and I now have a degree of admiration that I did not have previously.

SOMETIMES WHEN PEOPLE ARE TALKING TO ME about Mama, they say things like, "See, good things do happen to good people!" How I hope that somehow, somewhere, Mr. Reuben Cowart knows that he did a wonderful thing for a remarkable lady.

Epilogue

DADDY WAS SICK WHEN HE WROTE THE FOLLOWING letter to his oldest sister, Viola Ellis Hurlburt, but no one realized at that time that he would never be well again.

Centreville, Alabama
November 2, 1932
Dear Viola,

I had just about overlooked the request you made in your letter of July 10th for a poem dedicated to my dear Mattie until I was reading it over just a while ago. I am sorry that I have been so delinquent. It is not because I have not had the inspiration to write about my Mattie, but you know all of us great poets have our intermittent spurts at the game. I hate to turn out bad poetry on a poetry-loving race, and I just don't write unless I can write some that is first class.

Right now, with a touch of neuralgia, a bad cough, a stupid old gallbladder, and an empty pocket book, I fear that I am acting unwisely to undertake to write lines that will do justice to my dear sweet wife. Anyway, you may take the lines hereinafter inscribed and have Bertha try them out to some good

tune on the piano, or she can rub them across the washboard
and I'll turn out some better ones later on that will probably
find a place in your album of rare collections and wonders.
[Bertha, referred to in this letter, was Mrs. W. A. Gable, Viola's
daughter.]

My Mattie

You talk about your fluttering
and palpitating hearts,
A beatin' fast and faster still
All full of Cupid's darts;
But I can tell a story true
from first line to the last,
Of how my heart went tit-tat-too
One time back in the past.

My ducks had been to markets oft
And sometimes almost sold;
But always they would be brought back
For better bids to hold.
And I can thank my guiding star
Which led me safely by
For I just know I ne'er could beat
The one that caught my eye.

The things that others didn't have
To offer for my ducks
She seemed to have right from the first
And acme, prime, de luxe.
I viewed her hair of dark brown curls,
And feasted on her eyes.
Her smile just pierced my heart afresh,
Oh! how the arrow flies!

I went to work with all my might
    To win the prize I'd found,
New hat, new clothes, and brand new shoes,
    And candy by the pound.
A shave a day was not too much
    To keep me looking preened;
For I had found my Waterloo—
    My heart's long looked for queen.

She got a hold, no doubt of that,
    Upon my steel-cased heart,
For nothing that I thought or did
    Could stop the piercing dart.
Her smile was on my ledger's page;
    Her voice was in my room;
Her last sweet words rang in my ears
    To chase away the gloom.

When sleep was sweet and I at rest,
    She came into my dreams;
When sleep was past and I all drest,
    My joy flowed on in streams.
Of all the girls there was but one,
    I knew that I knew that,
So what was there for me to do
    But 'pop-the-question' flat?

So right away I went to work
    To make a pretty speech,
She must consent; I must not fail
    To get this lovely peach.
It worked—although I didn't use
    The speech made up before!

177

But what I said brought home the prize
   Delivered to my door.

Now we've been marching down life's lane
   Through thick and thin together,
A dozen years have all been spent
   And now almost another.
Since Hymen led us through his shrine
   And we became one flesh,
Each day brings forth a new-born joy
   And love springs forth afresh.

For better or for worse, we'll say
   She's mine forever more!
I'll keep my vows and she'll keep hers
   Up to bright Canaan's shore.
So here's my story, just in parts,
   Of how I got my Mattie;
To hear the rest (if I should tell)
   You'd doubtless call me 'batty.'

Daddy's letter to Aunt Viola continued—

I leave two weeks from today for conference—don't expect to be returned to Centreville. The family is tolerably well, except colds, etc.

                    Love to all,
                    Marvin

DADDY DID NOT LEAVE FOR THE ANNUAL Alabama Conference of the Methodist Church on November 16, 1932, as he had planned. Instead he went to bed with what he thought at first was flu. He was assigned to the Methodist Church in Eutaw,

Alabama, but he was sick when we moved there, and he never preached a sermon in the Eutaw Methodist Church. This was the beginning of the long illness which resulted in his death on Friday night at nine o'clock, March 31, 1933.

MAMA AND DADDY MARRIED ON HER twentieth birthday, February 19, 1920, so they were married for just over thirteen years when he died. She was a widow for over sixty years.

APPENDIX I
Copy

I, Reuben Adam Cowart, a resident of the City of Auburn, Lee County, Alabama, being over the age of 21 years and of sound and disposing mind and memory, do make, publish and declare this my last will and testament, in the manner following, to-wit:

1. I direct that all my debts, including my funeral expenses, expense of my last illness, and the expenses of the administration of my estate, be paid by my executor hereinafter named, out of any monies coming into his hands and available therefor.

2. After the payment of the debts and expenses referred to in paragraph 1 hereof, I give and bequeath unto Mrs. Mattie N. Ellis of Auburn, Lee County, Alabama, all my personal property, including money, stocks and bonds.

3. After the payments of the debts and expenses referred to in paragraph 1, and the payment of the legacy referred to in paragraph 2, hereinabove, I give, bequeath and devise all the rest and residue of my property of which I shall die seized and possessed, or in and to which I have any testamentary capacity or control, or whatever kind or nature and wheresoever situated, unto my mother, Mrs. Ellen Haynes Cowart, for and during the term of her natural life, and upon her death, the remainder to Mrs. Mattie N. Ellis of Auburn, Lee County, Alabama.

4. I hereby nominate and appoint my friend, Emil F. Wright, of Auburn, Alabama, the executor of this, my last will and testament, and exempt him from the giving of bond and from making any inventories to any court, and with power to sell so much of my personal property as may be necessary to pay the debts and expenses referred to in paragraph 1 hereinabove.

5. Lastly, I hereby revoke all former wills and codicils to wills heretofore by me at any time made.

IN WITNESS WHEREOF, I have hereunto set my hand and seal on this the lst day of July, 1943.

<u>/s/ Reuben A. Cowart</u>   (SEAL)

The foregoing instrument, consisting of this one page, was, at the date hereof, by said Reuben Adam Cowart, signed, sealed and published as and declared to be his last will and testament, in the presence of us, who, at his request, and in his presence and in the presence of each other, have signed our names as witnesses hereto.

   <u>Emil F. Wright</u>
   <u>Maiben H. Beard</u>
   <u>W. H. Sartin</u>

APPENDIX II

VENIRE FOR JURORS   AT LAW
THE STATE OF ALABAMA   CIRCUIT COURT OF LEE COUNTY
To any Sheriff of the State of Alabama—GREETING:

You are hereby commanded to summon the following named persons to appear at the courthouse, Opelika, Alabama, and serve as Regular Jurors at the Fall Term of the Circuit Court of Lee County, to-wit: Second week of Court, Tuesday, on the 19th day of November, 1963, at 9:00, A.M., they have been regularly drawn as Jurors for said Term of the Court.

NAMES	BEAT	OCCUPATION	RESIDENCE
James G. Brown	2	Merchant	Brown Grocery
Thomas C. Carr, Jr.	2	Western Rwy.	600 Crossley Dr.
Charles B. Collins	2	Salesman	Dairyland Farms
Isham J. Dorsey III	2	Ins. Salesman	608 N. 8th
W.D. (Bill) Dutton	2	Brick Contractor	Columbus Hwy.
Robert O. Floyd	2	Shop Foreman	Tatum Motor Co.
Harry Freisleben, Jr.	2	Merchant	Hagedorn's
Herbert Hard, Jr.	2	Orr Industries	India St.
Troy Hardy	2	Textile	Pepperell Mfg.
Paul Johnson	2	Asst. Co. Agent	Lee Co. Courthouse
L. C. Joiner	2	Oil Distributor	Standard Oil Co.
Carl Jolly	2	Textile	360 Pepperell
James M. Logan	2	Manager	Shelby Ave.
Billy James Martin	2	Textile	600 Lankford
L. J. (Bill) Morgan	2	Ins. Salesman	Claire Dr.
Noel Morgan	2	Salesman	Lee Co. TV Cable
Wm. C. McClendon, Jr.	2	Cleaners	Swiss Cleaners
G. S. (Shelly) Ross	2	Bookkeeper	1008 3rd Ave.
G. B. (Pete) Stough	2	NBC Salesman	310 North 1st
C. E. (Tot) Summers	2	Auto Salesman	Tatum Motor Co.
Guy Thompson	2	Electric Co.	Crossley Dr.
Bruce Trammell	2	Oil Co.	Lakeshore Blvd.
C. C. Wallace	2	Ins. Salesman	North 8th St.
Dewey Yancey	2	Salesman	Davis Dyar
Melvin Mayfield	4	Textile	Pepperell Mfg.
Eugene T. Conway	6	Farmer	Wire Road
Fowler Dugger	6	Newspaper	Wire Road
Marvin K. Gray	6	U.S. Postal	532 Dumas Dr.
Roy C. Luck	6	Mechanic	Moore's Mill Rd.

Thomas W. Lumpkin	6	Ext. Service	137 Nelocco Dr.
Fred P. Moore	6	Salesman	Moore's Mill Rd.
H. F. McQueen	6	Ext. Service	331 Hare Ave.
P. M. Norton	6	VA Coordinator	E. Magnolia Ave.
W. Fred Parker	6	Merchant	Parker's
James T. Reynolds	6	Engineer	364½ Payne St.
Hubert E. Self	6	Repairman	Ware Jewelers
Walter M. Crofton	7		Route, Opelika
James D. Watkins	7	Carpenter	Route, Opelika
J. Robert Bell	9	Gas & Oil	Rt. 1, Salem
Jack McConnell	9	Farmer	Rt. 1, Salem
Robert C. Littleton	9	Farmer	Rt. 1, Salem
Homer F. DuPriest	11	Merchant	Rt. 2, Salem
Wilbur Cooper	14	Serv. Sta. Owner	Rt. 2, Phenix City
Roy Ellis	14	Carpenter	Rt. 2, Phenix City
Allen Moon	14	Salesman	Smiths

From the 45 jurors listed above, the following twelve were selected—all white males:

Jury Foreman—Robert O. Floyd
(Shop Foreman at Tatum Motor Co.)
Charles B. Collins, *Salesman*
Isham J. Dorsey, III, *Insurance Salesman*
Herbert G. Hard, Jr., *Employee of Orr Industries*
Carl Jolly, *Employee of Pepperell Mills*
Jack McConnell, *Farmer*
L. J. (Bill) Morgan, *Salesman*
Shelly Ross, *Bookkeeper*
Bruce Trammell, *Trammell Oil Co.*
C. C. Wallace, *Insurance*
James D. Watkins, *Carpenter*
Dewey Yancey, *Salesman*

APPENDIX III

ANGEL FOOD CAKE
Preheat oven to 375°

1½ c. sugar	1¼ t. cream of tartar
1¼ c. egg whites	1 t. vanilla flavoring
1 c. + 2 T. cake flour	½ t. almond flavoring
¼ t. salt	

Place whole eggs (10 to 12, depending on size) in a bowl of hot water for at least 30 minutes. Eggs should be slightly warm. Separate eggs and place whites in large bowl. Add salt. Beat until foamy. Add cream of tartar and beat until whites stand in peaks, but are still moist and glossy. Add 1 cup of sugar (about ¼ c. at a time). Beat until stiff. Add flavorings and beat in well. Add flour, to which has been added the ½ c. sugar, sifted well together. Fold flour mixture in with a large slotted spoon in the same direction all the time, forward, over and under. Never stir round and round.

Pour in ungreased angel food cake (tube) pan and bake 25-30 minutes. When cake is slightly brown and loosening from sides of pan, it is done. Invert on cake rack to cool. To make the brown crust come out on the cake instead of sticking to pan, wring a cloth out in cold water and lay on bottom of inverted pan. Repeat several times as cloth becomes warm.

It is best not to use an electric mixture. Even the slowest speed will not result in as good a texture as a heavy hand and turned rotary egg beater.

ANGEL FOOD PIE
Preheat oven to 275°

1 prepared pie shell, baked	⅛ t. cream of tartar
4 egg whites (at room temp.)	1 t. vanilla flavoring
½ c. sugar	½ to 1 c. whipping cream
¼ c. sugar	

Beat egg whites with cream of tartar until slightly stiff. Gradually add ½ c. sugar, then vanilla and beat until very stiff. Pour into baked pie shell and bake in a very slow oven (275°) about 30 minutes until lightly browned. Cool, then refrigerate until thoroughly chilled.

Whip cream with ¼ c. sugar. Just before serving time spread whipped cream on meringue layer and decorate with strawberries, cherries, finely chopped pecans or walnuts, peaches, bananas, or other soft fruit or berries, fresh or frozen.

This makes a beautiful Christmas dessert when decorated with red and green Maraschino cherries, cut in halves or quarters.

OLD FASHIONED DARK FRUIT CAKE
Preheat oven to 275°

4 boxes (15 oz. each) raisins
2 c. Maraschino cherries (sliced with juice)
7 pints homemade preserves (pear, peach, fig, watermelon rind)
16 oz. chopped dates
1 pint jelly (apple, raspberry, grape, plum, or blackberry)
1 jar (16 oz.) strawberry preserves
1 small can frozen orange juice
1 small can frozen grape juice

12 c. chopped pecans (fewer if pecans are scarce and expensive)
3 well-rounded tsp. baking soda
2 lbs. oleo, melted
2 doz. large eggs, beaten with 2 c. sugar and 1 box brown sugar
11 cups plain flour, sifted with 1 T. salt; 4 heaping tsps. each ground cloves, baking powder, allspice, and ground cinnamon
pecan halves for decoration

Mix first nine ingredients and let stand overnight. Next morning, add soda and mix well. Add oleo, beaten eggs, and sugar. Sift dry ingredients together several times, then add to fruit mixture.

Line bottom only of pans with greased brown paper. Then grease and flour pan. Bake about 2 hours at 275°. Test with broom straw.

Remove from pans and peel paper off the bottoms.

This makes about 35 pounds and may be baked in tube or loaf pans. Pans should be filled only about half full. I use 6 angel food cake pans (one for each of my children) and 2 large loaf pans.

I mix this in a #1 zinc tub.

APPENDIX IV

The first three verses of the poem, which was embroidered in the appropriate squares of The Quilt, were written by our Grandfather, Gabriel Richard Ellis when our older sister and Grandpa's namesake, Gay, was born December 6, 1920. The last five verses were added by Daddy after the rest of us were born:

> Howard, January 31, 1923;
> Norman, December 11, 1924;
> Wesley, April 4, 1927;
> Carolyn, April 25, 1929;
> Lamar, April 21, 1931.

One dark and dreary stormy night,
When neither moon nor stars gave light,
Old Mother Stork came rolling 'round
With a tiny babe to Ridertown.

"This babe," said she, "Two hearts must fill
with joy, who live on yonder hill";
So ere the night did pass away
She gave to them sweet little Gay.

And gently laid her by the side
Of Marvin's dear little black-haired bride,
And said to them, "Be good and true
To this little babe I give to you."

The stork came back a few more times
And made me feel like writing rhymes,

To let the world know just how happy
A man can be when he's called "Pappy."

The next who came right after Gay
Was Howard Marvin full of play.
Then came Norman two years later
'Bout as long as Grandpa's gaiter.

Next came Wesley, full of frolic,
Singing a tune of midnight colic.
Carolyn came in two years more
Which brings the list to one-and-four.

When the sixth one came around
We just knew that we had found
The sweetest yet to see the light
In our home so glad and bright.

But, "honest-injun," all are sweet,
Not a one can e'er be beat
By any babe in any home
In any clime or any nome.

APPENDIX V

Recital de
ORGANO

Organista: Wesley Ellis
Sabado 16 de Noviembre de 1991
7:30 de la noche
CATEDRAL METROPOLITANA

I

Dietrich Buxtehude
(1637-1707)
Praeludium, fuge und Ciacona

Georg Phillip Telemann
(1681-1767)
Schmucke dich, o liebe Seele

Johann Sebastian Bach
(1685-1750)
Chorale Preludes:
Wachet auf, ruft uns die Stimme
Nun Komm' der Heiden Heiland
In Dir ist Freude

Sebastian Duron
(murio despues de 1716)
Gaitilla de mano izquierda

II

Cesar Franck
(1822-1890)
Chorale in A Minor

III

Robert Powell
(1932—)
Four Psalm Preludes:
23-The Lord is my Shepherd
29-Ascribe Unto the Lord, Ye Mighty
137-By the Waters of Babylon
*117-O Praise the Lord, All Ye
Nations*

Marcel Dupre
(1886-1971)
*Antiphon III-I am black but comely,
O Ye Daughters of Jerusalem*

Charles Ives
(1874-1954)
Adeste Fidelis

Sigfrid Karl-Elert
(1877-1933)
Choral Improvisation on Nun Danket

INDEX
Italicized number indicates photograph
Asterisk indicates fictitious name

191